Maximising the Impact of Teaching Assistants

Teaching assistants have become an integral part of classroom life, yet pioneering research by the authors has shown that school leaders and teachers are not making the most of this valued resource. Results from the Deployment and Impact of Support Staff (DISS) project showed that the more support pupils received from teaching assistants, the less academic progress they made. Yet it is not decisions made by the teaching assistants themselves, but decisions made by school leaders and teachers about how their support staff are used and prepared, which explain these provocative results.

Prompted by the wake-up call the DISS project findings provided, this timely book of guidance will help school leaders and teachers in primary and secondary schools improve the way they use teaching assistants, and will add real value to what can be achieved in the classroom. Based on the authors' collaborative work with schools in the Effective Deployment of Teaching Assistants (EDTA) project, this book provides essential, practical tools and classroom-tested strategies that will allow schools to conduct a fundamental review of current practice. It also provides a unique framework for reforming teaching assistant deployment and preparation.

Maximising the Impact of Teaching Assistants provides much-needed and well-informed guidance on how to unleash the huge potential of teaching assistants working in schools and is essential reading for all school leaders.

Anthony Russell was a researcher at the Institute of Education, University of London, UK, and has previously worked as a teacher, science adviser and deputy director of the APU science team at King's College, London, UK.

Rob Webster was a researcher on the DISS and EDTA projects at the Institute of Education, University of London, UK, and has previously worked as a teaching assistant in mainstream and special schools.

Peter Blatchford is Professor in Psychology and Education at the Institute of Education, University of London, UK, and directed the DISS and EDTA projects.

Maximising the Impact of Teaching Assistants

Guidance for school leaders and teachers

Anthony Russell, Rob Webster
and Peter Blatchford

Routledge
Taylor & Francis Group

LONDON AND NEW YORK

First published 2013
by Routledge
2 Park Square, Milton Park, Abingdon, Oxon OX14 4RN

Simultaneously published in the USA and Canada
by Routledge
711 Third Avenue, New York, NY 10017

Routledge is an imprint of the Taylor & Francis Group, an informa business.

British Library Cataloguing in Publication Data
A catalogue record for this book is available from the British Library.

Library of Congress Cataloging in Publication Data
Russell, Anthony, 1942-
Making the most of teaching assistants : guidance for school leaders and
teachers / authored by Anthony Russell, Rob Webster, Peter Blatchford.
p. cm.
ISBN 978-0-415-66127-0 (hardback) -- ISBN 978-0-415-66128-7 () -- ISBN
978-0-203-06928-8 () 1. Teachers' assistants. I. Webster, Rob, 1976- II.
Blatchford, Peter. III. Title.
LB2844.1.A8R87 2014
371.14'124--dc23
2012030932

ISBN: 978-0-415-66127-0 (hbk)
ISBN: 978-0-415-66128-7 (pbk)
ISBN: 978-0-203-06928-8 (ebk)

Typeset in Galliard
by Saxon Graphics Ltd, Derby

MIX
Paper from
responsible sources
FSC
www.fsc.org   FSC® C013056

Printed and bound in Great Britain by
TJ International Ltd, Padstow, Cornwall

Contents

Introduction   1

1   The case for change: Implications and strategies   10

2   Auditing the deployment, preparation and practice of TAs   19

3   The deployment of TAs   41

4   The preparedness of TAs   70

5   The practice of TAs   87

6   Conclusions   99

Appendices   102
Notes   110
References   111
Index   113

Introduction

This book is a guide to help practitioners who want to rethink the use of teaching assistants (TAs). In this introduction we give the background to the book.

The Deployment and Impact of Support Staff (DISS) study

The DISS study (2003–2008) was designed to help fill gaps in knowledge of TAs' deployment and impact. There were two broad aims:

1 To provide an accurate, systematic and representative description of the types of support staff and their characteristics and deployment in schools, and how these changed over time.
2 To analyse the impact of support staff on teachers, teaching and pupil learning, behaviour and academic progress. The study focused on all types of support staff and all pupils.

This was the largest study yet undertaken on support staff and involved a large-scale nationally representative questionnaire survey involving nearly 18,000 responses from headteachers, support staff and teachers; detailed analysis of the effect of TA support on the academic progress of 8,200 pupils; detailed systematic observations, work pattern diaries and transcripts giving systematic accounts of TA activities and interactions; and in-depth case studies. The findings received wide media coverage and the results are also summarised in our recent book: *Reassessing the Impact of Teaching Assistants* (Blatchford, Russell and Webster 2012).

Findings on the impact of TA support on pupils' learning

The DISS project found that the effect of TA support on pupils' academic progress is at variance with the positive views of teachers about their impact. The study assessed the effects of TA support on pupils' academic progress in English, mathematics and science. Two 'waves' (or cohorts) of pupils in seven age groups across the primary and secondary years were tracked from the beginning to the end of the school year. The results were striking. Of the possible 21 results (there were 7 age groups and 3 subjects), 16 were in a negative direction. These results stood, even when accounting for the factors that are known to affect academic progress and the allocation of TA support, such as prior attainment and level of special educational needs (SEN). Importantly, there were no positive effects of TA support for any subject for any year group.

To summarise, pupils receiving the most TA support made less progress than similar pupils who received little or no TA support – even after controlling for factors likely to be related to academic progress and the allocation of TA support (e.g. prior attainment and SEN status).

The DISS results were a 'wake-up call' and they made it clear that urgent action now needs to be taken to address the way TAs are used in schools. In our book *Reassessing the Impact of Teaching Assistants*, we explain that the fault does not lie with individual TAs, but with decisions made about how TAs are used, albeit with the best of intentions, by schools and teachers. We also developed the 'Wider Pedagogical Role' (WPR) model to both summarise findings from the DISS project and to suggest possible explanations for the results on academic progress. The WPR model enables us to interpret the impact of TA support on pupils' academic progress within the wider context of the factors within which TAs work, and which, we argue, maximises or inhibits their effectiveness, and over which they have little or no control.

We unpack the WPR model in more detail in Chapter 1. However, it is necessary for what follows in this chapter, to say something about its three main components. First, there is the *preparedness* of TAs and teachers, which covers: (i) their training for their respective roles (for teachers, this will influence how they make the most of TAs in their classrooms, and for TAs, training will influence their pedagogical and subject understanding); and, (ii) the amount of planning, preparation and debriefing/feedback time available for teachers and TAs. The second component, the *deployment* of TAs by teachers and headteachers, concerns which pupils TAs are allocated to work with; typically, this will be individuals and groups of lower-attaining pupils and those with SEN. And finally, the *practice* of TAs concerns the nature and quality of their interactions with pupils, which we found to be far less academically demanding and task-driven, compared with teacher-to-pupil interactions. These factors, working in combination, which govern TAs' employment and deployment, offer the most fruitful answers to questions about the effectiveness of TA support.

In the *Reassessing the Impact of Teaching Assistants* book we concluded that a fundamental rethink is required in the way TAs are used in order not to let down supported pupils, and the book sets out the case for this practical handbook, using the WPR model as an organisational framework.

The Effective Deployment of Teaching Assistants (EDTA) project

Following the DISS project we conducted a project funded by the Esmée Fairbairn Foundation in which we worked with schools and teacher and TA pairs in two local authorities in England. This project was invaluable as a way of developing and evaluating alternative ways of using TAs that worked for schools and for pupils, and which dealt with the negative impact of TAs identified in the DISS project. We will describe this project in more detail in the next chapter. The EDTA project was supplemented by extensive discussions with headteachers, teachers and local authority staff with responsibilities for the TA workforce and for pupils with SEN during the numerous Inset and consultancy activities that we have undertaken since the publication of the DISS project findings. Our work was also informed by the work of Prof. Michael Giangreco of the University of Vermont, USA, and his colleagues, as well as other commentators and researchers.

As a result of this work, it was strongly felt that a book with guidance on the effective deployment of TAs would be extremely helpful to headteachers and class teachers who are interested in understanding and improving the ways in which they deploy TAs across schools and within classrooms.

Key features of this book

This book is intended to give guidance to help primary and secondary schools with the management and deployment of TAs, following the huge rise in support staff in UK schools over recent years. It goes beyond previous guidance, and shows the need for a fundamental rethink of the current use and purpose of TAs, based on results from the largest study worldwide on TA impact – the DISS project.

This book includes advice and case studies based on extensive collaborative work with local authorities, schools, headteachers, teachers, special educational needs co-ordinators (SENCos) and TAs, and has undergone extensive trialling in schools through the EDTA project. The guidance, as well as the structure of the EDTA project itself, is underpinned by a conceptually and empirically strong model, developed to explain the DISS project findings.

We offer alternatives to common but, we argue, mistaken methods of TA deployment, which are currently letting down lower-attaining pupils and those with SEN. We draw out recommendations for practice at the school and classroom level, and for policymakers nationally. We also anticipate that this book will be of international significance, at a time when more and more countries are introducing TAs to mainstream classrooms.

Finally, we have written this book in such a way as to be accessible to practitioners, with many examples and tools for use in professional development and in-service training.

Although there have been a number of practical guides to the use of TAs, this book is different because it is based on results from a research project which, for the first time, studied in detail the impact of TAs on pupils and teachers. The DISS study was, we feel, unique in terms of its scale, its scope, its timeliness, its systematic, representative data, its mixed method approach and its relevance to policy. The coherent story which was constructed from the careful integration of the various sources of data was further extended and validated by the EDTA project, which developed and evaluated the efficacy of the WPR model.

The aim of this book is therefore to complement our book, *Reassessing the Impact of Teaching Assistants*, by providing essential practical information and tools to allow schools to conduct a fundamental review of current practice and provide a framework for reforming methods of TA deployment. We feel that existing guides on the use of TAs are now outdated if they serve to maintain the status quo and fail to recognise and address the central problem identified by the DISS research. Current methods must be re-evaluated in order to realise the huge potential of the many TAs working in mainstream schools.

And it is not only the TA's role that will be informed by a serious attempt to deal with the DISS findings:

The school's role

The key driver for change is the school itself. Our view, based on extensive visits to schools and discussions about this topic, is that if you are a headteacher or senior leader you need to fundamentally review how your school deploys TAs, what expectations you have of them, and, crucially, you need to then lead change. We have often found that headteachers – and many others in education – see the truth in our findings, and are willing to consider the implications for their schools. But too often we have found that action is delegated to middle leaders, not necessarily connected to, or reporting directly to, the senior leadership team (SLT). This can mean change is piecemeal and sometimes puts the staff who have been delegated the responsibility for change in a difficult position, particularly if change requires amending employment contracts (e.g. in terms of hours of work). So change needs to be sanctioned and led from the top by the headteacher and SLT members. The DISS findings on the impact of TAs show that this is not an option, but a necessity.

The teacher's role

One of the things to emerge from the DISS and EDTA projects is the way that change is also required in the teacher's role. In particular, if you are a class teacher you will have to work through a more inclusive pedagogical strategy, which deals with the learning of *all* pupils, and not delegate the day-to-day responsibility for the learning and care of pupils with SEN and lower-attaining pupils to TAs.

Let us be clear: retaining the status quo, in terms of the current and widespread models of deploying TAs, is letting the most vulnerable children down. Current practices must be re-evaluated in order to realise the huge potential of the many TAs working in mainstream schools.

Readership and purpose of this book

Readership

As we mentioned above, it is our experience that work on rethinking the use of TAs will not be successful if non-senior staff are given the job of co-ordinating action in primary and secondary schools. For this reason the book is primarily directed at *headteachers* and other members of the SLT, in both primary and secondary schools, as you are the key decision-makers from whom the impetus and plans for change must come.

This is *not* a book written for TAs, though hopefully they will find much of great relevance and they will obviously be involved in the process of change. Instead, this book is directed at those who make strategic decisions about the best ways of deploying TAs.

Our experience is that schools can use a re-examination of the role of TAs as a valuable exercise in school improvement more generally, because the effective use of TAs also overlaps and connects with the effective use of teachers, school management structures, school resources, provision for pupils with SEN, and so on.

Class teachers are the second group at which this book is directed, as they have the day-to-day responsibility for deciding how to make the most effective use of the TAs with whom they work. We present the material in this book in terms of a nested approach: it is within the context of the school-level decisions made by the SLT that teachers make their classroom level decisions about TA deployment.

The book will also be highly relevant to SENCos and inclusion managers, who, depending on the size of the school they work in, may also have a teaching or senior leadership role. It should help with strategies designed to include pupils with SEN in mainstream schools and it helps address issues associated with the use of interventions to boost pupils' progress. It is designed to help with wider ambitions that form the basis for school improvement.

The results from the DISS project made it clear that teachers are given very little guidance on working with TAs through either the initial teacher training (ITT) course or school induction. Given that we also found that virtually every teacher works with a TA, this is a lamentable state of affairs, and so this book provides material for ITT staff and students, and trainees who are taking school-based routes to qualified teacher status (e.g. the Graduate Teacher Programme). The book is also relevant to foundation degree courses. Additionally, it supports a range of professional development Inset courses, seminars and consultancy sessions on the use of TAs in schools.

More widely, decision-makers at the regional and national level who are concerned with policy and practice regarding support staff in mainstream schools (both in the UK and in countries where TAs are prevalent in schools) will also find the book of great relevance to their work.

Purpose

This book has been designed to provide easy-to-use, evidence-based materials and activities to improve the preparation of TAs and teachers, the deployment of TAs, and TAs' interactions with pupils.

A main aim of the DISS and EDTA projects was to learn lessons, identify good practice and collect examples from schools for inclusion in this book. We offer solutions and strategies developed in the studies, as well as: accessible summaries of key recommendations, examples of strategies successfully used in schools, and much-needed examples of effective practice in the form of short case studies.

This work also describes a school-based methodology or audit for self-evaluation: approaches, techniques and factors to consider when making an in-house assessment of TA preparation and deployment, and the provision for pupils with learning needs. The audit engages stakeholders in a dynamic process of review and performance improvement, identifying and building on existing good practice. The aim is that schools will be able to use this as a template for undertaking an audit of provision as well as developing solutions and strategies for change. This guidance has credibility because it is based on the experiences of practitioners and genuine trials in schools.

The aim of the audit process is to determine the extent to which the reality matches participants' perceptions, and to provoke discussion about how models of deployment and preparation could be modified and improved.

We anticipate that once this process has started, schools will want to continue to evaluate their practice, and refine and develop new strategies in the light of new challenges. Overall, the book has the components to encourage reflective practice and continued school improvement.

It is our experience that there is no 'one size fits all' solution; as a school, you will need to arrive at local solutions to the general problems we have identified through the DISS project. To this end, examples of work already conducted in schools should be of value to those seeking to rethink the use of TAs.

The book contains numerous suggestions about working at the *school level* for SLT, and at *classroom level* for teachers working with TAs. As noted above, these suggestions will also be of immediate use to others in a variety of contexts, such as SENCos and trainee teachers.

The overall standpoint of the book is to sympathise with those headteachers and teachers who told us that their schools would struggle to function without TAs, but to show why progress can only be made if we first recognise that there is a problem with the current and widespread forms of TA deployment, and that alternative ways of utilising them need to be developed.

Our recommendations deliberately address the fact that schools – especially given the impact of the recent global economic downturn – are unlikely to receive any additional funds from government in the immediate future with which to implement workforce employment and deployment decisions. It was therefore within the context of schools operating within already stretched budgets that we worked in collaboration with schools to develop, and then evaluate, creative strategies to TA deployment and preparation in the EDTA study. In some ways this may be more productive in the long run as it can lead to more profound and longer-term changes; schools in the EDTA project decided to rethink and change existing ways of operating, rather than adopt additional practices that require short-term funding and thus are short-lived.

We continue to conduct consultancy work and give presentations on the role and impact of TAs, and the results from the DISS and EDTA studies have been invaluable in providing a wealth of material to help you deploy your TAs more effectively. This book is an attempt to share this work more widely.

Using this book

Whether you are a headteacher looking for guidance on remodelling your TA workforce or a teacher looking for techniques and strategies to improve your own classroom practice with regard to TA deployment and preparation, there are some things you should consider in order to support your use of this book.

Headteachers and school leaders

If you, as a headteacher, have picked up this book with a view to reforming the way you use TAs in your school, we would first like to commend you for taking this matter seriously. No doubt you will already be aware that this is no small task, but, as we have been emphasising in this opening section, it is a vital one if schools are to make the most of their TAs and have a positive rather than detrimental impact on pupil learning. Therefore, before we go any further, it is worth sharing some of the experiences of the senior leaders who took part in the EDTA project who were once at the start of this journey.

Through the EDTA project, we were able to work with staff in schools who were convinced of the need for change and willing to undertake the developmental work on which wider practice could be built. In any work of this nature, it is worth identifying the members of an organisation who support the main vision and are willing to contribute actively to developing and testing new ideas as part of a change team. Having a small core of enthusiastic colleagues who are open to new ways of working with TAs – including TAs themselves – can be vital in not only testing out new ideas in the classroom, but also becoming advocates of change among your wider staff team, championing new ideas and getting colleagues on board. If possible, and if relevant, aim to get representation from staff working in each key stage. The value of informal ways of gathering grassroots support for change cannot be overestimated.

Many of the schools we worked with in the EDTA study had regular SLT meetings dedicated to this work, and one primary school formed a cross-school working party comprising the headteacher, SENCo, a senior teacher and a higher-level teaching assistant (HLTA), who met termly to plan action and discuss progress.

It was also through the experience of participating in the EDTA project that school leaders reached the conclusion that change takes time. In the project, we had three terms in which to plan, pilot, develop and evaluate the trials that schools introduced. It was the view of some of the senior leaders that this is a project that cannot be rushed, and that three terms is about right for conducting the groundwork for wider whole-school change. Be sure to set aside regular time through the year to focus on your own project. This process of change should not be an 'add on' to other activities; it is a serious and systematic approach to whole-school improvement.

The timing of introducing whole-school change is important too. A number of headteachers said that it would have been difficult to introduce some changes during the school year. Spending a full school year planning, developing and evaluating meant that they were able to hit the ground running come the start of the next school year.

In the EDTA project, schools spent each term working on trials connected to one of the three main components of the WPR model: deployment, practice and preparedness. Participants told us that this helped to focus attention on particular areas. We recommend that schools using this book adopt a similar approach, and indeed, we have structured this book in a way that prioritises the order in which the WPR components should be addressed as part of your restructuring (see chapter summaries below). Following the model used in the EDTA study, for each term's work, whatever the focus, you will need to plan, prepare action and run trials. Towards the end of each term, you should evaluate what was done, and feed in the conclusions to your change plan for the next school year.

The spirit in which any process of change regarding the role of TAs is carried out in schools is often important to its success. We do not need to remind you that these are sensitive times: we are reminded daily of high unemployment, public sector spending cuts and the pressures on low- and middle-income families. This is no time or environment in which to conduct a process that will have staff members fearing that it could lead to redundancies. We do not recommend that this book be used as part of a staff rationalisation or competency process. It is important that all school staff realise that the process described in this book is a valuable exercise to inform whole-school improvement. The aim is to evaluate school processes that enable and inhibit TAs from performing their role effectively. You should be aiming to identify and build on what works well in schools and move towards the kinds of practice that can unlock the massive potential of TAs.

While the EDTA project did not ask schools to examine their SEN provision *per se*, it is worth mentioning that the review of TA employment and deployment that participants undertook inevitably raised questions about the ways in which schools meet the needs of pupils with SEN. The role of the TA has become deeply connected to service delivery for SEN, but as the DISS project has shown, there are inherent risks in assuming TAs are either the *only* option or the *appropriate* provision. Therefore, the audit and processes of change described in this book could be conducted as part of, or alongside, a wider review of school structures and processes connected to SEN provision. Alison Ekins' book, *The Changing Face of Special Educational Needs* (2012) provides a useful starting point.

Key recommendations

- Form a cross-school change team to plan and conduct trials in classrooms, and feed back their experiences.
- Have regular SLT and change team meetings to discuss and evaluate the trials, and to feed this into the development of your school policy on TA deployment.

- Take a school year to conduct this preparatory work and be ready to start the next year with a full school-wide roll-out of new strategies.
- Be clear about your motivations for conducting this process. Reassure TAs that it is not an assessment of how well they do their job, but an evaluation of how effectively the school supports them.

Teachers

You may, of course, be a class teacher – perhaps an experienced practitioner, a newly qualified teacher (NQT) or a trainee – and are thinking about ways in which you can improve your own classroom practice with regard to TA deployment and preparation. Although it is primarily intended for school leaders, you do not have to be working in a school that is planning to review and change TA deployment at the organisational level to make use of the material in this book. There is advice and strategies for implementation at the classroom level that can improve not only the way you use the TA(s) you work alongside, but can also help you to add value to your teaching. We would encourage you to read Chapter 1 and think about how you can appraise your own current practice before applying new strategies and models of working.

Trainers

One of the main findings from the DISS project was that despite TAs' high visibility in classrooms, 75% of teachers reported having had no training to help them work with TAs as part of their pre-service training and professional development. This points to a clear challenge for ITT and we would anticipate that teacher trainers, plus those involved in the delivery of continuous professional development, would be able to use material in this book to inform course content. This book and its companion volume – *Reassessing the Impact of Teaching Assistants* – may well be considered key texts on trainees' reading lists. It could also be considered essential reading for SENCos undertaking the National Award.

Contents of the book

Chapter 1: The case for change: Implications and strategies

This chapter sets out the case for rethinking the current and widespread ways of using TAs. We provide an explanation for the negative relationship between TA support and pupil progress found in the DISS project using the Wider Pedagogical Role model, and raise questions for readers to think about. We explain how the WPR model provided the structure for the EDTA study intervention and how we formally evaluated the project.

Chapter 2: Auditing the deployment, preparation and practice of TAs

This chapter aims to raise your awareness of the need to review the deployment, preparation and practice of TAs as they are currently in your school, and to guide you on the tools through which the present situation in any one school and/or class, or across the schools in one area (e.g. a cluster), can be obtained. We draw on the audit devised as part of the EDTA project and through which we confirmed its usefulness in helping schools to initiate the processes of review and change.

Chapter 3: The deployment of TAs

The perceived role of the TA is central to the ways in which they are deployed, and this chapter will set out the various roles assigned at the school level by headteachers and at the classroom level by individual teachers. The linking – or 'Velcroing', as it is sometimes known – of TAs to pupils with SEN and those whose attainment is relatively low, will be presented as the central issue about TAs facing the SLTs and teachers. The DISS project has shown that, at present, decisions regarding TA deployment are often detrimental to the pupils being supported, so change is clearly necessary.

Chapter 4: The preparedness of TAs

This chapter deals with this component of the WPR model at two levels: the school and the classroom. The school level will include issues such as: induction; TAs' pedagogical and subject knowledge and skills; training; recruitment; and contracts. At the classroom level, the main focus will be on issues of time for TAs to meet teachers for preparation and feedback on a day-to-day basis, as well as communication more generally.

Chapter 5: The practice of TAs

The verbal interactions between TAs and pupils ('practice' in our terms) are at the heart of their role as supporters of learning. This will be the focus of Chapter 5. Although this obviously relates to decisions and strategies at the classroom level, there are school-level decisions relating to strategic choices about questioning styles, monitoring and training, which can be made to improve TAs' practice. Furthermore, it reveals ways in which schools and teachers can reduce the need for adult support by helping pupils to develop independent learning skills.

Chapter 6: Conclusions

In this final short chapter we sum up with some general conclusions about the impact of carrying out the suggestions in this book, based on the experiences of schools who have worked with us on rethinking their use of TAs.

Chapter 1

The case for change
Implications and strategies

Background

The increase of TAs

One of the most profound changes in UK schools over the past 15 years or so has been the huge and unprecedented increase in support staff in schools. The number of full-time equivalent (FTE) TAs in mainstream schools in England has more than trebled since 1997 to about 190,000 (DfE 2011). At the time of writing, (summer 2012), taken together, TAs[1] comprise 24% of the mainstream school workforce in England, Wales and Scotland[2]: 32% of the nursery/primary school workforce; and 15% of the secondary school workforce (DfE 2012b; Statistics for Wales 2011; The Scottish Government (2011). Only 6% of TAs in England and Wales have higher-level teaching assistant (HLTA) status.

Perhaps not surprisingly, such a substantial part of the school workforce accounts for a significant proportion of the annual education budget. Expenditure on TAs in 2010/11 constituted 16% of the £17.1 billion spent by primary schools, and 10% of the £16.5 billion spent by secondary schools (DfE 2012a).

The rise in TAs is part of a general increase in education paraprofessionals with similar roles worldwide. Giangreco and Doyle (2007) found increases in support staff are reported in schools in Australia, Italy, Sweden, Canada, Finland, Germany, Hong Kong, Iceland, Ireland, Malta and South Africa, as well as the USA. TAs, therefore, appear to be a growing part of the school workforce in many countries, although this has been more pronounced in the UK.

Several developments over the mid-to-late 1990s have driven this growth, including greater numbers of pupils with SEN in mainstream schools, and the introduction of the national literacy and numeracy strategies. From 2003, the number of TAs (and other support staff) increased further following the implementation of *The National Agreement* – a policy response to problems with teacher recruitment and retention. The Agreement had the twin aims of raising pupil standards and tackling excessive teacher workload via new and expanded support roles (DfES 2003a).

The findings from the DISS study show that the general effect of these initiatives has been that TAs now occupy a role in mainstream schools where they interact with pupils – principally those not making expected levels of progress and those with learning and behavioural difficulties. On the face of it, this may look to you to be a good arrangement, because they provide more opportunities for one-to-one and small group work both in and out of the classroom. However, as we have seen, it has also led to negative consequences for supported pupils.

This evolution of the TA role profoundly changed the dynamics of classroom interaction, and has to a large extent occurred with little debate or public discussion, or research on the impact of TA support on pupil learning. Most of the existing research on TAs suggests a generally positive view about their function in schools. The increase in TA numbers has proceeded largely on the ungrounded assumption that they help to raise standards for pupils. While there is evidence that TAs have a positive impact on teacher workloads and stress levels (Blatchford, Russell and Webster 2012), until the DISS project, there was next to no research on the impact of TAs on pupils over sustained periods (e.g. a school year) and under everyday classroom conditions. Such evidence as exists tends to be derived from small-scale intervention studies, involving specific subjects and/or year groups (see Alborz *et al.* 2009).

Accounting for the negative relationship between TA support and pupil progress: the Wider Pedagogical Role model

In order to explain the negative relationship between TA support and pupil progress, we might reasonably assume that pupils who were given most TA support in the first place would have been those most likely to make less progress in any case. However, such explanations, in terms of pre-existing characteristics of pupils, are unlikely because such factors that typically affect progress (and TA support), such as SEN status, prior attainment and measures of deprivation, were controlled for in the statistical analyses. To be of any consequence, any potential factor causing or influencing this relationship would need to be systemic across *all* year groups and *all* subjects, and related to *both* pupil attainment *and* the allocation of TA support.

Another possible explanation for the negative relationship is that it may be due to the different levels of TAs' qualifications relative to teachers. We note, however, that research has not found that teachers' or TAs' level of qualification are related to their effectiveness (Blatchford *et al.* 2004, Muijs and Reynolds 2001, Wiliam 2010).

So, if pupil factors and TA qualifications do not appear to be explaining the negative relationship between TA support and pupil progress, what is?

We argue that it is the decisions made by headteachers and teachers that govern TAs' employment and deployment, which offer the most fruitful answers to this question.

We developed the Wider Pedagogical Role (WPR) model to explain the DISS project results and also to provide the basis for our recommendations to you regarding the role and use of TAs, as set out in this book. The basic components of the WPR model are shown in Figure 1.1 (taken from Blatchford, Russell and Webster 2012). We will go on to present the key findings from the DISS project thematically, using the three main components of the WPR model: *deployment, preparedness* and *practice*.[3] For each component, we raise questions and points of discussion for you to think about in relation to the situation in your school or classroom.

Deployment

The findings on deployment led us to some stark conclusions about the role of TAs. It is clear from work pattern diaries, systematic observations and interviews we conducted that TAs have a direct pedagogical role, supporting and interacting with pupils, and this exceeds time spent supporting the teacher and curriculum, or performing other tasks.

Is this the case in your school?

What is more, results from detailed observations showed that teachers tended to interact with pupils in whole-class contexts and infrequently worked with them on a one-to-one basis or with groups. In contrast, TA-to-pupil interactions, both in and away from the classroom, tended to be with individual pupils or small groups.

Do you know if this general finding matches what happens in your school?

Results were also clear about which pupils TAs supported. The majority of TA support, both in and away from the classroom, was for pupils failing to make the expected levels of progress or those identified as having an SEN (including those with a statement of SEN). Teachers provided less support to these pupils than did TAs, and TAs hardly ever supported average- or higher-attaining pupils. Crucially, we found that TA interaction with pupils increased, and teacher interaction decreased, with the severity of pupils' SEN.

Is this how TAs are deployed in your school?

The types of interactions with teachers and TAs also differed. Pupils were nine times more likely to have sustained interactions with TAs than with teachers. 'Sustained' means that the pupil was the focus of the TA's attention for longer than the length of the observation interval (ten seconds). Furthermore, pupils were six times more likely to be actively involved in their interactions with TAs than with teachers. Here, 'active' involvement is defined in terms of beginning, responding to or sustaining an interaction with an adult during the observation interval. In contrast, for the vast majority of their interactions with teachers, pupils were one of a crowd.

Do you know if this is what happens in your classrooms?

This kind of one-to-one support from TAs might seem pedagogically valuable, but there are serious and unintended consequences. A main consequence is that supported pupils become separated from the teacher, missing out on everyday teacher-to-pupil interactions. Further, as many TAs are given the responsibility for planning and leading interventions (e.g. for literacy), often away from the classroom, TA-supported pupils also spend less time in mainstream curriculum coverage. This is particularly the case for pupils with SEN: TAs have, in effect, become the primary educators of these pupils, and the impact of TA support on their academic progress is much worse.

Are you surprised by these results?

Preparedness

Preparedness describes two aspects of TAs' work:

- The training and professional development of TAs and the teachers (e.g. how teachers manage and organise the work of TAs).
- Day-to-day preparation (e.g. time for joint planning and feedback between teachers and TAs).

Teacher and TA training

Given the growth of TAs and their high visibility in classrooms, it might be expected that training to help teachers work with TAs would form part of pre-service and/or Inset training. However, the DISS project surveys of teachers showed that 75% of them reported having had no such training. This was despite the fact that over the duration of the study, the proportion of teachers involved in directly training TAs grew, so that by the end of the study, over half of teachers were involved in such training.

What kind of preparation, if any, have your teachers had to work with TAs?

The surveys also revealed that over half of teachers and SENCos line managed one or more TAs. Yet, again, two-thirds of these line managers had not received any training for this role. Teachers who had received training in relation to working with and/or line managing TAs reported mixed views. For both types of training, the majority of respondents said it lasted only one day or less, and only half rated the training as useful.

How have your teachers been prepared for such an extension of their role?

Day-to-day preparation

The second aspect of preparedness concerns how TAs are prepared to support pupil learning. One of the DISS project's key findings was that 75% of teachers reported having no allocated planning or feedback time with the TA(s) they worked with. This was most marked for secondary schools, within which 95% of teachers claimed that they had no such time. Communication between teachers and TAs was largely ad hoc; conversations took place during lesson changeovers, before and after school, and during break and lunch times, and so, for the most part, relied on the goodwill of TAs.

Are arrangements in your school better than this typical situation?

In interviews, many TAs reported feeling underprepared for the tasks they were given. With little or no time to talk with teachers before lessons, TAs described how, in many cases, they had to 'tune in' to the teacher's delivery in order to pick up vital subject and pedagogical knowledge, and information and instructions relating to the tasks they supported pupils with.

Have you ever tried to find out how your TAs feel about their levels of preparedness?

Practice

The DISS project findings on 'practice' (i.e. the interactions between TAs and pupils) make it clear that pupils' one-to-one interactions with TAs are not only longer, more sustained and more interactive compared with their interactions with teachers, but these interactions differ in *quality*.
  There were three overarching characteristics of TAs' talk to pupils:

1   TAs' talk to pupils was frequently more concerned with *task completion* than with ensuring that any learning and understanding had taken place.

2   TAs' interactions with pupils could be broadly characterised as *reactive*, because – unlike teachers, who guided lessons with planned learning aims in mind – TAs had routinely to respond to the needs of the pupil(s) and the lesson in the moment.
3   Teachers generally '*open up*' pupil talk, whereas the TAs '*close down*' the talk, both linguistically and cognitively. TAs, therefore, do not tend to know how to make the best use of the extended, more frequent interactions they have with pupils.

Have you ever listened to a TA teaching a pupil?

The Wider Pedagogical Role model

We can now see that the DISS project findings suggest three main explanations for the troubling and unexpected findings on the impact of TA support on pupil learning:

1   Despite much debate about the appropriate role of TAs, they now have a predominantly pedagogical role, directly interacting with pupils (principally those with learning needs). As a consequence, such pupils become separated from the teacher and the curriculum.
2   There are severe limits in terms of the preparedness of teachers and TAs in terms of their training to work together, and the amount of time they get to discuss pupils and lesson tasks.
3   The interactions of TAs (practice) with pupils are less academically demanding, with a stress on completing tasks rather than ensuring any learning or understanding takes place.

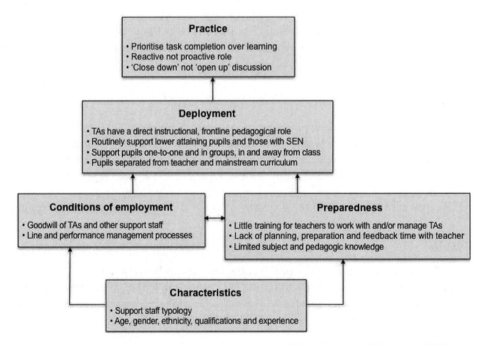

Figure 1.1 The Wider Pedagogical Role model (from Blatchford, Russell and Webster 2012)

We developed the Wider Pedagogical Role model to explain the troubling results on pupil academic progress found through the DISS project. The WPR model sets TA effectiveness (in terms of pupil outcomes) within a wider context, which takes account of the factors that govern their employment and deployment, and over which they have little or no control. The model, presented in full in Figure 1.1, shows the key findings from the DISS project and how the components of TAs' work relate to one another.

The Effective Deployment of Teaching Assistants project

This book is based on work conducted as part of the Effective Deployment of Teaching Assistants (EDTA) project. This one-year action research project gave us the opportunity to support the development of more effective models of TA usage in primary and secondary schools.

The idea for the EDTA project emerged following discussions with a set of small working groups which we (the research team) held after the DISS project findings were published in autumn 2009. The groups were comprised of headteachers, local authority advisers, teacher/TA trainers and SENCos. (We did not include TAs in these groups because the purpose was to develop a dialogue with staff with decision-making responsibilities at the school and classroom level.) We worked with the groups in a deliberative inquiry, exploring the key components of the WPR model and defining its utility and relationship with classroom practice.

The working groups confirmed our belief that there was a pressing need for clear, well-informed guidance on effective ways of deploying and preparing TAs and teachers. To this end, we bid for, and were successful in getting, funds from the Esmée Fairbairn Foundation to conduct an intervention project to address this issue.

The aims of the EDTA project were:

1   To work with headteachers, teachers and TAs in order to develop effective school-based strategies for TA deployment in primary and secondary schools.
2   To evaluate the strategies and models of practice, and the processes by which they are introduced and developed, describing what worked well in the local implementation process.

The intervention

Schools in two local authorities (LAs) in England were approached to participate in our intervention project, which lasted the duration of the 2010–11 school year. Two pairs of teacher-TA teams were recruited from ten schools (six primary and four secondary). Visits were made to the school before the end of term in the previous school year to meet the participants, plus headteacher or SENCo, to explain involvement in the study.

At the beginning of the school year (September 2010) we held meetings for school leaders, SENCos and teachers in each LA, at which we presented in full the DISS project findings, plus the rationale and aims of the present study. We also hosted two meetings for TAs to impart the same information.

A key feature of the EDTA project was the way in which we used the three core components of the WPR model as focal points for each term of the school year. We began with preparedness in the autumn term; addressed deployment after Christmas (spring term); and following Easter (summer term) schools focused on practice. Schools were encouraged to develop trials relating to the focus for that term, which would address one or more pertinent issues that arose from the DISS project. At the LA meetings with school leaders, SENCos and teachers, we set out the particular problems with existing models of TA preparation. Staff from each school then developed one or two trials to undertake for the rest of the term. The trials were set out on a pro forma for reference, and copies made for each school and the research team.

Similar LA meetings were held in December 2010 and April 2011, at which school staff discussed and developed trials on, respectively, the themes of deployment and practice. As with the post-DISS project working group meetings, we did not include TAs in the LA meetings because, as stated already, we believe that change has to come from those with decision-making responsibilities.

Halfway through each term, a member of the research team visited the school to observe and discuss with each teacher-TA pair the progress of the trial they had been working on.

The evaluation

We adopted a within-school comparative approach to the evaluation, evaluating practice before and after the introduction of the development trials. The evaluation compared new models developed through trials, with existing models of TA deployment and teacher-TAs working together. The main question addressed was whether involvement in the proposed project led to more effective deployment, preparation and practice of TAs.

In early September 2010, we sent each participant a copy of an audit (one each for school leaders/SENCos, teachers and TAs). Each audit presented a set of scenarios on a sliding scale, describing situations drawn from the DISS study, and which could be broadly defined as ranging from 'ineffective' to 'effective' practices. Respondents were asked to identify which scenario matched their own experiences or perceptions. Teachers and TAs were also asked to estimate the proportion of time they spent working in particular contexts (e.g. supporting groups; working one-to-one with a pupil; leading the whole class, etc.).

In order to see whether there had been any change over the year, researchers visited each school in September and again in the summer term, towards the end of the school year, in addition to the half-termly visits noted above. The data collection tools used in this study were based on the reliable and tested methods used in the DISS study, and combined quantitative structured observations (in two-minute blocks) with qualitative data drawn from semi-structured interviews and general observations.

At the beginning and end of the school year, researchers undertook structured observations of at least one lesson per teacher-TA pair. This was followed up with an interview with each individual participant. Researchers used the interviews to discuss points of interest on the audit (e.g. where the teacher's response to one question was markedly different to the TA's response, and vice versa) and to obtain more detail on things seen in the observations. Data were analysed to see how perceptions matched the reality in the classroom from the perspective of people at three levels (school leaders/SENCos, teachers and TAs). These findings were illustrated with comments drawn from transcriptions of the interviews and the open-ended questions included on the audit.

In addition to this more formal evaluation, researchers asked teacher-TA pairs to evaluate the success of the trials they had undertaken during the discussions held as part of the half-termly visits to schools. The discussions with teacher-TA pairs also explored the nature of any facilitative or inhibiting factors to the successful implementation of the trials. For example, a number of secondary school staff felt that a lack of time prevented them from fully enacting some of their trials. Although frustrating for the participants, these experiences were nonetheless valuable in terms of helping us to understand the wider contexts in which change does or does not happen in schools. All of these experiences were collated and fed back to participants at the termly LA meetings (e.g. the feedback on the first trials on preparedness were fed back at the end of the autumn term, in December 2010).

At the final LA meeting, we met with school leaders, SENCos and teachers in order to feed back on the final development trials on practice, and also to provide a briefing and discussion on the overall project findings. We also met with the TAs to feed back and discuss the project findings.

Key findings

The findings from the EDTA project provide the evidence for the material presented in this book. We summarise some of the main project findings at the end of Chapters 3, 4 and 5, in order to show you how the guidance collated in this book changed things in schools and classrooms. We present a summary of overall findings from the EDTA project in Chapter 6 and in Webster, Blatchford and Russell (2012). The full final report (Blatchford, Webster and Russell 2012) is available from our website, www.schoolsupportstaff.net. However, as we build the case for change, it is worth sharing some of the key findings here.

As a result of participating in the intervention:

- Teachers were more aware of their responsibilities towards lower-attaining pupils and those with SEN, and worked more often with these pupils.
- There were improvements in the quality of TAs' interactions with pupils.
- Schools created teacher-TA liaison time.
- Teachers provided TAs with clearer and more detailed lesson plans.
- TAs' esteem, value and confidence improved from having a more clearly defined role.

Perhaps the key message from the EDTA project for school leaders and teachers is this: changing the way you prepare and deploy TAs is not only possible, but has significant benefits for *all* school staff and *all* pupils.

Rethinking policy and practice on TAs: the political and educational context

The EDTA project has extended the messages arising out of DISS project and has given fresh impetus to policy changes. Our work on TAs has informed the Lamb Inquiry on parental confidence in the SEN system and recent guidance to Ofsted inspectors with responsibility for assessing SEN (Ofsted 2011); we shall highlight where this has been the case at relevant points throughout the book. The DISS study has also influenced the present UK coalition government's 2011 Green Paper on SEN. While we welcome the fact that the government addresses the contribution of TAs and other support staff to the education of pupils with SEN, we are concerned that it does not offer any challenge to the status quo in terms of how TAs are deployed in support of pupils with such needs. We are deeply concerned that the failure to engage fully with the fundamental questions raised by the DISS project will reinforce current models of practice, which continue to let down disadvantaged children. In the current political climate, change seems ever more likely to be delegated to individual schools, and so it is our belief that our work will be of great assistance to headteachers looking for a framework for change.

There is a wider educational consideration here. We know that lower-attaining pupils, as well as those with SEN, tend to be supported by TAs rather than teachers. As has been argued in the USA by Giangreco *et al.* (2005), an implicit form of discrimination has developed: the most vulnerable and disadvantaged pupils receive less educational input from teachers than other pupils. If there are grounds for saying that pupils with SEN are not appropriately served by this arrangement, there are also grounds for saying that lower-attaining pupils are equally poorly served.

If we are therefore serious about addressing the well known 'tail' in educational (under) performance, then we should take very seriously the experiences of lower-attaining pupils and those with SEN, and the way in which current methods of deploying TAs may not be helping their educational progress as much as we may have thought.

An extreme take on the DISS project findings on pupil progress, as described in our book, *Reassessing the impact of Teaching Assistants*, could be to cut drastically the number of TAs in schools. However, schools have much to gain from TAs, and few, if any, would wish to lose them. We agree with the sentiment we hear time and again from headteachers who tell us that without TAs, their school would not function successfully. Reframing the purpose and role of TAs is therefore essential in order to avoid wasteful expenditure and a negative impact on pupils, with the added advantage of giving TAs their own identity and value, which is demonstrable through a measurable impact on pupils.

To restate a central message from the DISS project: the reasons why support from TAs has a negative effect on pupil progress is not the fault of individual TAs; it is due to the systemic decisions made at school and classroom level, by school leaders and teachers – not TAs – about how TAs are deployed and prepared.

The unintentional drift towards the situations revealed by the DISS project (e.g. TAs becoming the primary educators of lower-attaining pupils and those with SEN) arguably owes much to a lack of direction from government. In this sense, there are key messages for policymakers beyond the school level.

We believe it is important to move forward in order to establish clear roles for teachers and TAs, and produce the systems to support and maintain the demarcation, so that each role – though different and complementary – is valued and respected on its own terms. It is also our strong belief that it is schools that are best placed to undertake this work. When they do, as the overarching message from the EDTA study shows, change *is* possible.

To be successful, however, schools need clear, well-informed guidance. This book benefits from and builds on the work achieved by schools in the EDTA project in order to provide such guidance. In the absence of a clear steer from government and central agencies on how to go about this, we feel our book fills a vital gap. It provides much-needed guidance, based on authentic and credible work conducted in schools and classrooms.

The overall challenge for you (which this book supports) is to define the role of the TA and show how it adds value to pupils' educational and social development in a distinctive way. We suggest the strategy of first envisaging the classroom as it would be with the teacher, but without the TA, and then making decisions about how the teacher would need to organise things in order to provide the best educational experience for *all* pupils in the class. Following this, the TA could then be introduced back into the classroom, so to speak, in such a way that they then provide an additional resource. This would help identify ways in which the TA adds value to what the teacher provides, rather than replacing the teacher.

Chapter 2

Auditing the deployment, preparation and practice of TAs

Introduction

This chapter covers the rationale for and process of an audit of the current models of TA deployment, preparation and practice in your school. While this chapter is intended for school leaders at the first stage of undertaking the fundamental rethink of school-wide TA usage, there are useful ideas that can be easily adapted by individual teachers seeking to appraise and develop their own classroom practice regarding TAs.

Why conduct an audit?

Our extensive research into the deployment and impact of TAs has shown that the inadvertent effects of TA support are inextricably linked to the decisions made about TAs' deployment and preparation. These decisions, made with the best intentions, do not lie within the control of TAs, but instead with school leaders and teachers.

Yet, as the DISS project findings revealed, the impressions school leaders and teachers had about the effectiveness of TA deployment, preparation and practice were at variance with the objective measures of TA impact. In short, what school leaders and teachers *believed* to be effective ways of using TAs, were in fact – pedagogically speaking – doing more harm than good.

For this reason in particular, it is important that, before any changes are made, you obtain as full a picture as possible of how TAs are currently deployed and prepared in your school, and of the nature of their interactions with pupils, via an audit of your teaching and TA staff. It is likely too that, given the well-forged links between TA deployment and processes of inclusion for pupils with SEN, an audit of TA usage will provide an additional commentary on how effectively the school and teachers meet the needs of lower-attaining pupils and those with SEN.

The results of a TA audit will provide you with a starting point in terms of identifying the areas requiring change and the extent to which it is needed. These results will also act as a baseline against which you can evaluate change at a later date, using the same tools. The auditing process is also valuable in terms of identifying areas and examples of good practice on which to build.

What should the audit cover?

In line with our Wider Pedagogical Role (WPR) framework, we recommend structuring an audit around the three dimensions of TA deployment, preparation and practice. We will highlight some specific areas within each dimension that you should aim to cover in your audit, along with some suggestions about the type of tools that can be used to collect data. The examples in this chapter are based on tools used in our research, the reliability and validity of which have been tested through years of fieldwork. We provide photocopiable versions of the main tools in the Appendices. There are also blank copies of the tools to download from our website. Go to www.schoolsupportstaff.net and follow the link to *Maximising the Impact of TAs*. However, you should choose the auditing methods best suited to the questions you want to answer, and in this sense, our instruments can be used as templates for you to adapt.

You should aim to collect data that provides both an objective and subjective picture of current practice. As we have noted, it is important to get a clear sense of the extent to which: (i) what you *think* is happening in classrooms across the school matches the reality; and (ii) your perceptions of what is happening (and their effects) are shared by your staff. A further point to consider, therefore, is how different parts of the audit link together. As you will see, it is possible, via the audit, to obtain a picture of TA deployment and practice that moves from the broad school level, through the classroom level, right down to the fine detail of the pupil experience.

As we explained in the Introduction, in line with the way the responsibility for supporting the needs of lower-attaining pupils and those with SEN has shifted away from teachers towards TAs, TAs are very often handed the duty of planning, delivering and assessing curricular interventions. Based on the experiences of schools that participated in the EDTA project, we argue that there is much to be gained from a parallel review of interventions, in terms of the impact they have on pupil progress. We will say more about this in later sections of the book, but for now, it is worth having in mind what a systematic evaluation of interventions (especially those delivered by TAs) would add to your audit of TA deployment.

Conducting the audit

As a school leader you will no doubt be alert to the sensitivities involved with conducting an audit of working practices. An underlying sense of judgement can sometimes accompany such an exercise, particularly one that involves TAs – a group of the workforce unaccustomed to the type of evaluative processes more readily associated with teachers.

It is important to emphasise that any judgements that may be made on the basis of the audit findings primarily reflect the historic decisions made and actions taken (or, indeed, decisions *unmade* and actions *not* taken) by the school leadership team and teaching staff, and are not a reflection of the competency of individual TAs. We recommend that you undertake the audit in a transparent way and that the messages about what is being judged (e.g. decisions and processes), and what the potential impact of the audit might be, are clear to TAs. You may like to meet with your TA team and describe the rationale and audit process, gaining their cooperation and support.

TAs should not feel pressured into participating in the audit, or made to feel that it is something that is 'being done to them'. In particular, it should be stressed that the audit is *not* a staff rationalisation or competency process; that is to say, it is not being conducted in order to make judgements about the effectiveness of individual TAs and/or their continued employment. TAs should be made aware that they are contributing to a valuable exercise to inform whole-school improvement, and one that, based on the findings of the EDTA study, we would argue has considerable benefits for TAs.

Features of the audit

The deployment of TAs

There are two levels at which you should examine the deployment of TAs: the school level and the classroom level. The latter is nested within the former, thereby providing a view on how the current models of TA deployment are played out in classrooms.

TA deployment at the school level

As the person responsible for setting and overseeing the whole-school vision for the overall use of TAs, you will want to know if school staff share this vision. Or, if you have a current policy on TA deployment, you will want to know the extent to which it is adhered. You should seek to obtain a broad level view of the tasks performed by TAs in terms of the extent to which TAs:

- Work in and away from classrooms
- Lead whole classes (perhaps as part of lesson cover arrangements)
- Provide pastoral support to pupils (e.g. supporting physical needs; pupil welfare; assist with social interaction; mentoring; dealing with behaviour)
- Perform non-teaching tasks (e.g. classroom display; preparing resources; filing; tidying up)
- Prepare for, deliver and/or assess work for intervention or booster sessions
- Meet with teachers to plan and prepare
- Meet/liaise with parents and outside agencies.

In the DISS project, we used a 'work pattern diary' to obtain general information on the main activities of TAs. We provided a form listing the most commonly performed tasks, and asked TAs to tick which tasks they carried out in 20-minute periods across one school day. The data was collected anonymously.

Such an analysis at the school level is powerful in terms of revealing not only the frequency but also the amount of time spent on different activities. We recommend that you conduct a similar survey. You might like to base your version on the task category system we used in the DISS project. A complete list of the individual activities, grouped into six main categories, is provided in Table 2.1.[4] In the DISS project, the data was collected on just one day, but you may wish TAs to complete such a diary over a week. Furthermore, TAs could be asked to record tasks performed during hours for which they are in school working, but for which they are *not paid* (e.g. before or after school).

Methods such as the work pattern diary above can help you to derive a systematic picture of school-wide TA deployment, but you may also wish to gather data on the *perceptions* of TAs on the ways in which they work. One way in which you might gather such information is via a questionnaire, structured around the categories and tasks listed above. You could apply a scale to some or all of the tasks and ask TAs to indicate the extent to which they perform or are involved in them. An example is shown in Table 2.2 for the tasks relating to supporting teachers and the curriculum.

Table 2.1 Typical TA tasks for school-level audit of TA deployment

1. Support for teachers/curriculum
Classroom preparation including display
Clerical support (e.g. worksheet preparation)
Give feedback to teachers
IEP development and implementation
Participate in development of lesson plans
Prepare and maintain equipment/resources
Provide advice and guidance for teachers
Record-keeping
Support and use ICT

2. Direct learning support for pupils
Deliver lessons (covering teacher absence)
Deliver learning activities
Deliver interventions/booster programmes
Give feedback to pupils
Managing pupil behaviour
Perform pupil assessments (e.g. for SEN)
Provide specialist pupil support
Reward pupil achievement
Supervise pupils out of class
Support excluded pupils
Support for pupils to achieve learning goals
Support pupils to understand instructions

3. Direct pastoral support for pupils
Attend to pupils' personal needs
Develop one-to-one mentoring
First aid/pupil welfare duties
Help pupils make informed choices
Pastoral support for pupils
Provide specialist pupil support

4. Indirect support for pupils
Interaction with parents/carers
Monitor and record pupil progress
Record-keeping

5. Support for school (admin/comms)
Admin tasks (e.g. ordering materials)
Carry out reception/telephone duties
Clerical/admin/general office support
Dealing with school correspondence
Facilities/premises/lettings/marketing
Financial admin (e.g. payroll, school budget)
General school administration
Liaise with agencies/external professionals
Interaction with parents/carers
Liaise between teaching and support staff
Operate attendance/pastoral systems
Participating in stock ordering/auditing
Provide advice/guidance to staff and pupils
Record-keeping
Support and use ICT

6. Support for school (environment)
Arrange storage of stock and supplies
Assist teachers with health and safety
Other duties arising from use of premises
Carry out minor repairs
Ensure standards of cleanliness maintained
Ensure pupils' toilets properly maintained
Ensure security of premises and contents
Maintain a good working environment
Maintain and distribute stock and supplies
Maintain/check/repair equipment
Monitor and manage stock and supplies
Monitor work by outside agencies
Operate equipment
Participate in stock storage/ordering/auditing
Receive and distribute deliveries
Remove and rearrange furniture

Table 2.2 Example of question for TAs regarding their support for teachers/curriculum

Using the scales on the right, indicate the extent to which you are in involved in the following tasks, which support teachers and the curriculum.	*Little or no involvement*	➔		*High involvement*	
Classroom preparation including display	1	2	3	4	5
Clerical support (e.g. worksheet preparation)	1	2	3	4	5
Feedback to teachers	1	2	3	4	5
IEP development and implementation	1	2	3	4	5
Participate in development of lesson plans	1	2	3	4	5
Prepare and maintain equipment/resources	1	2	3	4	5
Provide advice and guidance for teachers	1	2	3	4	5
Record-keeping	1	2	3	4	5
Support and use ICT	1	2	3	4	5

The role and purpose of TAs – and teachers

It was our experience in the EDTA project that teachers find it hard to comment on TA deployment to the same detailed level and with the same confidence as TAs. Task audits, similar to that above, completed by teachers for the EDTA project produced less reliable data or no data. Therefore, we were unable to include much of it in the analysis that contributed to the project evaluation. The reasons for this are understandable: the TAs whom teachers were asked to comment on, especially those in secondary schools, were often deployed to work across several classrooms with several different teachers, or to work outside the class beyond the sight of teachers. Teachers did not have as full a picture of TA deployment as TAs themselves did.

Nevertheless, it is important for you as a school leader to obtain a clear picture of teachers' perceptions of how they deploy TAs, and we will cover the methods by which these data can be collected.

It is equally important to establish a cross-school view of teachers' perceptions of the role and purpose of TAs, as well as the perceptions of TAs themselves. It is important that you establish any misconceptions about the TA role, which can be addressed ahead of the discussions and actions that will bring about change. As you begin to think about how you can establish a clearly defined role for TAs – which is different from, but complementary to that of teachers – you should aim to find out the degree to which your staff members feel the teacher and TA roles overlap and/or are distinct. There are several methods that are useful for gathering such information.

Questionnaires (especially if completed anonymously) allow individual teachers and TAs to articulate their understanding of and views about the role and purpose of TAs, and what the school expects from them. Therefore, it may be necessary to include in the audit open and closed questions relating to the issue of role clarity, for example:

- What are the main responsibilities in your role as a TA in this school?
- Describe how your role as a TA differs from the role of a teacher?
- Are there any ways in which your role as a TA is similar to the role of a teacher?
- Describe the ways in which the role of the TA is distinct from your role as a teacher?
- Do you have any views about the similarities and/or differences between the teacher and TA role?
- Do you have any views about the ways in which TAs are deployed?

As well as obtaining written information from individuals via questionnaires, you might like to consider the use of focus groups. You could establish two groups – a teacher group and a TA group – and task each group with establishing the criteria that define their role and contribution. To allow an open discussion and ensure participants are not inhibited in their responses, you should arrange for them to meet alone, without SLT present. The list of criteria that each group produces will ensure a level of anonymity for individuals.

Our research has uncovered worrying evidence about which members of staff have the responsibility for pupils with SEN (Webster, Blatchford and Russell 2012). There was a view among secondary school teachers that meeting the needs of pupils with learning and behavioural needs is the responsibility of the Learning Support department, where TAs are based and where pupils with SEN go to do curriculum interventions. Where the common practice was to attach a TA to a pupil(s), this led to teachers passing the responsibility for instruction or differentiating material for these pupils to TAs.

Case study

Consulting TAs

To encourage openness and honesty, teachers in one primary school interviewed each other's TA. TAs were asked the same set of questions. They appreciated being asked for their views. Teachers described the process as 'very revealing', as the process uncovered a wide range of perceptions and ideas about the TA role. The consultation showed a lack of a common understanding of the TA role, and initiated a much-needed discussion about how to establish consistency.

Given the well-documented association between TAs and pupils with SEN, the issue of who has responsibility for pupils with SEN should be addressed in your audit. Ask teachers and TAs what they perceive as their respective roles and responsibilities in relation to the school's provision for pupils with SEN by adding some neutrally worded, open-ended questions to the questionnaire, for example:

- *How would you describe your role and responsibilities in meeting the needs of pupils with SEN?*
- *If you are a TA, what do you identify as teachers' main responsibilities for meeting the needs of pupils with SEN?*
- *If you are a teacher, what do you identify as TAs' main responsibilities for meeting the needs of pupils with SEN?*
- *What are your views on how effectively the school meets the learning needs of pupils with SEN?*

The auditing process will produce two sets of data – one from teachers and one from TAs – reflecting:

- Teachers' and TAs' understanding of and views about their respective roles
- Teachers' understanding of and views about the TA role
- TAs' understanding of and views about their own role
- Views of the extent to which the teacher and TA roles are distinct
- Teachers' and TAs' understanding of their own and each others' role and responsibility for pupils with SEN.

These data can be analysed and put together with your own understanding of the role(s) and purpose(s) of TAs; here, we are asking that you conduct some form of audit of the views held by you, your SLT and your SENCo (if he/she is not a member of the SLT) on this topic. We are aware of some school leaders who have made use of official documentation that formally set out the teacher and TA roles in order to inform their audit. The Qualified Teacher Status (QTS) standards, standards for obtaining HLTA status, and TA role profiles produced by local authorities (which outline the key responsibilities and entry level requirements for TAs at three or four different levels) are useful for establishing the demarcation between the teacher and TA roles.

TA deployment at the classroom level

As part of your audit, you must also obtain a detailed picture of the current models of TA deployment at the classroom level. This information will form a core part of the basis for review and change. In our experience, this is where the most revealing data about TA deployment – and teachers – will be found. Yet the TA's role in a lesson is only one side of the coin. The role of the teacher must also be considered because, as we have explained, decisions they make about TAs have implications for the ways in which teachers organise their *own* work (e.g. in terms of which groups of pupils they work with). Teachers involved in the EDTA study told us that they found the auditing process productive as it provoked them into thinking about the models of classroom organisation they use, and in many ways had taken for granted. Thinking about the ways in which they deployed TAs led them to reflect helpfully on their own practice.

We recommend that you gather subjective views from individuals (e.g. via a questionnaire) and a more objective method, specifically classroom observations. We will consider the use of both methods, starting with some ways in which you can survey your staff.

SURVEYING TEACHERS AND TAs

In the EDTA study we used an audit to gather subjective data from teachers and TAs on their perceptions of the extent to which they;

- worked with pupils on a one-to-one basis or with groups of pupils,
- worked with higher-, average- and lower-attaining pupils, and those with SEN,
- roved (walked around) the classroom, perhaps in a monitoring role,
- led or addressed the class,
- did other tasks, such as: preparing resources; marking pupil work; tidying up; or administrative tasks.

And, for TAs only, the extent to which they;

- listened to the teacher teach (e.g. were part of the class audience).

We give two examples of survey questions addressing these contextual situations (Tables 2.3 and 2.4). For both questions, respondents (teachers and TAs) are asked to consider the occasions throughout a typical week when they work alongside each other in the classroom. Because of the limited knowledge teachers have of contexts where TAs work away from them, out-of-classroom situations need to be handled separately.

As we have mentioned, our experience in the EDTA project of asking classroom teachers to describe what TAs do when they are working *outside* the classroom (and therefore out of teachers' direct supervision) produced limited or even missing data, because they do not observe these situations and were thus less confident about their estimates. For this reason, it may not be possible to include the level of detail we suggest in Table 2.5 in surveys to be completed by teachers; however, they should be asked to provide an outline of their understanding of how TAs are deployed away from their classroom in a typical week. You could obtain this information via an open-ended question, such as: *in a typical school week, describe how TAs are deployed by other teachers in other classrooms/departments elsewhere in the school.*

Table 2.3 Example of survey question on adult deployment in classrooms 1

During a typical school week, estimate the proportion of time (as a %) that you spend doing the following. Only provide a percentage score for item 6 if you are a TA. Ensure that your percentages add up to 100%.	
1) Working with a pupil one-to-one	%
2) Working with a small group (up to 5 pupils)	%
3) Working with a larger group (between 6 and 10 pupils)	%
4) Roving the classroom	%
5) Leading the class	%
6) *(TAs only)* Listening to teacher talk to the class	%
7) Other (please specify)	%
Total	100%

Table 2.4 Example of survey question on adult deployment in classrooms 2

During a typical school week, estimate the proportion of time (as a %) that you spend doing the following. Ensure that your percentages add up to 100%.	
1) Supporting higher-attaining pupils	%
2) Supporting average-attaining pupils	%
3) Supporting lower-attaining pupils	%
4) Supporting pupils defined as having SEN (e.g. those with a statement of SEN)	%
5) Supporting mixed attainment groups	%
Total	100%

For TAs, then, much of what has been described in Tables 2.3 and 2.4 can be applied to contexts where they work with pupils away from the classroom; for example, in the learning support department, inclusion unit, withdrawal area or a specialist provision. We provide examples of survey questions addressing the ways in which TAs are deployed away from mainstream classrooms in Tables 2.5 and 2.6. For both questions, TAs are asked to consider the occasions throughout a typical week when they work away from the classroom and teachers.

Table 2.5 Example of survey question on adult deployment away from classrooms 1

During a typical school week, estimate the proportion of time (as a %) that you spend doing the following. Ensure that your percentages add up to 100%.	
1) Working with a pupil one-to-one (e.g. leading an intervention)	%
2) Working with a group of pupils (e.g. leading an intervention)	%
3) Working with pupil(s) in a pastoral/welfare context (e.g. mentoring; physio)	%
4) Preparing, planning and/or assessing pupil work (including for interventions)	%
5) Doing administrative tasks (e.g. photocopying or filing for teachers; display)	%
6) Other (please specify)	%
Total	100%

Table 2.6 Example of survey question on adult deployment away from classrooms 2

During a typical school week, estimate the proportion of time (as a %) that you spend doing the following. Ensure that your percentages add up to 100%.	
1) Supporting higher-attaining pupils	%
2) Supporting average-attaining pupils	%
3) Supporting lower-attaining pupils	%
4) Supporting pupils defined as having SEN (e.g. those with a statement of SEN)	%
5) Supporting mixed attainment groups	%
Total	100%

The process of surveying teachers and TAs in this way will reveal the proportion of time teachers and TAs estimate that they each spend working in particular contexts with particular groups of pupils in the classroom and, for TAs, the proportion of time they spend doing specific activities when working away from the classroom. We also advise including spaces on the questionnaires you devise for respondents to add any additional information, which may help explain or expand on their responses. We have collated the questions in Tables 2.3 to 2.6 in a photocopiable pro forma in Appendix 1. A blank version can be downloaded from our website.

These detailed classroom level data can be examined alongside the school-level data about the purpose and role of TAs, confirming and/or contradicting the overall picture presented by these subjective views. However, to add an extra layer of meaning to the audit process, it is necessary to supplement these data with data from classroom observations.

Case study

A process of 'finding out'

The teachers in one primary school conducted a small-scale audit of their TAs, with the aim of ensuring that the teachers made best use of the TAs' time. The teachers drew up a comprehensive list of the tasks TAs performed (e.g. supporting an individual pupil; working with a small group; roving around the classroom; preparing resources, etc.) in different parts of the lesson. TAs were asked to rate on a five-point scale how often they thought they spent time doing those tasks (e.g. very frequently, frequently, sometimes, rarely or not at all).

The teachers developed this checklist into a simple observation schedule, which the TAs completed for one another. Particular attention was paid to the TA role during teacher input, group work and plenary.

The TA-completed checklists and observations were followed up with discussions between each teacher/TA pair, in which the TAs were asked about the different tasks they did during the lesson. This in turn led to a conversation about how the TAs could make best use of their time in lessons and the TAs identified the following: making notes on teacher input for later use with groups; monitoring pupils' reactions for signs of understanding or confusion; and encouraging pupils to contribute to class discussions.

We found that for the classroom teachers who participated in the EDTA project, asking them to provide accurate estimates of the proportion of time TAs spent working in particular contexts with particular individuals and groups (in terms of attainment level) was not as straightforward as it was for TAs. This was largely because the TAs were out of the teachers' sight for parts of the week, and so they had a partial picture of how TAs spent their week.

For this reason, and for reasons connected to obtaining more objective data, we strongly recommend conducting observations of TAs in action throughout the school, working in classrooms alongside teachers, and away from classrooms with individuals and groups of pupils.

The value of using lesson observations in order to generate a deeper understanding of classroom processes is well known, and indeed, the DISS project relied heavily on the use of observational data in order to build a systematic, moment-by-moment description of how TAs and teachers were deployed in classrooms and the roles they undertook. It was in the light of the findings from the lesson observations in particular, that we were initially able to make sense of the troubling results on pupil progress.

We provide a simplified version of the tried and tested lesson observation schedule used in the EDTA project in Table 2.7, which we present as a worked example to make clearer its intended use. We have completed the sheet using data from an actual classroom observation conducted as part of our research. A blank photocopiable version of the observation pro forma is available in Appendix 2, and can also be downloaded from our website.

The lesson observation schedule is designed to help you not only derive a clear systematic picture of how TAs are deployed in classrooms and what roles they undertake, but further, to obtain an understanding of how teachers make use of TAs (especially with regard to meeting the needs of lower-attaining pupils and those with SEN) and how their own pedagogical practice is affected by the presence and deployment of a TA.

We suggest that observations are conducted by members of SLT who are part of your project change team. We also recommend that you observe all of your TAs at least once, and observe lessons in their entirety.

The process for completing the observation schedule is straightforward. With reference to Table 2.7, you will notice that the schedule has been designed to allow a TA's activities to be recorded on a minute-by-minute basis over a one-hour lesson.

The second column is for you to log the phase of the lesson in progress (e.g. teacher's main input, main learning task and plenary). A point raised by our research concerns the fact that the way in which lessons are structured affects the TA's role. For example, TAs often spend the teacher input stage listening to the teacher – in effect, being part of the class audience; during the main learning task, they mostly work with individuals or groups; and while the teacher is leading the plenary, TAs often gather in books and resources or tidy the room. This is by no means to say that this is what goes on in every lesson in every classroom, but it is, in our experience, commonplace and worth drawing to your attention. The rationale for including the lesson part in the observation is to help you obtain a picture of the TA role during key parts of the lesson. These data may reveal broad patterns of TA deployment across the school.

The five columns grouped under the heading '*Predominant activity of TA*' are used to summarise the main role the TA had during each minute of the lesson; that is, what he/she did for 30 seconds or more (Please note: these 30 seconds do not have to be consecutive).

You could summarise TA activity every second minute if you prefer, using the alternately shaded rows as a guide (e.g. indicating the predominant TA activity over a two-minute, rather than one-minute block). However, for your analyses to be meaningful, you will need to be consistent across all observations.

The total number of ticks per column should be entered in the bottom row (*Total ✓*). This can be converted to a percentage of the total per observation to summarise the main activities of the TA (*Summary*). In the worked example in Table 2.7, the TA worked with pupils on either a one-to-one or group basis for the majority of the time (53% cumulatively), and listened to the teacher teach for a third of the lesson (35%). Such data becomes very meaningful when aggregated across a greater number of observations.

The four wider columns on the right of the schedule allow you to add qualitative notes on the pupil(s) with whom the TA works (*TA-supported pupil(s)*), and any evidence of the extent to which the tasks the TA supports pupils with have been differentiated, or are different, from the tasks undertaken by the rest of the class.

General notes on the *teacher's role* and interactions with pupils at significant points in the lesson are also helpful, as they will reveal similarities and differences between the two roles. You can use the time intervals in the left-hand column to make these notes at concurrent intervals.

Those of you who are confident in using this kind of observation method may wish to use another observation schedule to collect concurrent data about the prominent role of the teacher at one or two minute intervals. In this way, you can perform an analysis that allows you to make a comparison of teacher and TA activities in the classroom, as we did in the EDTA project (Blatchford, Webster and Russell 2012).

The last column on the observation schedule (*Features of TA-to-pupil talk*) can be used to record key features of the TA's talk in line with the time points from the observation. This is also why noting the lesson part is useful, as you can generate a fairly reliable picture of the TA role and the types of TA talk at different phases of the lesson. For example, what the TA says to pupils when sitting beside them during the teacher's main input, or when working with a group during the main learning task. These notes can be made with reference to the directory of the common features of TA talk shown in Table 2.8. TA-to-pupil interaction is covered in detail in Chapter 5.

We strongly recommend, too, that you observe TAs in two other contexts, if relevant to current deployment practice in your school. First, you should observe TAs when they lead classes. The DISS study revealed that some schools used TAs as part of their arrangements for covering planned and unplanned teacher absence, and also to free up time for teachers' planning, preparation and assessment (PPA) time. These greater responsibilities represent a significant development in the history of the TA role, as they bring the TA to the front of the class in ways not seen before. As part of your audit, it is essential for you to know how effectively TAs who are given this role manage classrooms and deliver lessons. The observation schedule in Table 2.7 can easily be used to collect these data.

The second context in which you should observe TAs is when they are working away from the classroom, delivering interventions with individuals and groups. Again, you can use the observation schedule to collect these data; however, our experience of observations of this kind suggests that it will be much more meaningful for you to take qualitative notes of such sessions, paying particular attention to TAs' interactions with pupils.

Table 2.7 Worked example of lesson observation schedule, adapted from version used in the EDTA project

| Date: 17/09/12 | Teacher: R. Lee (RL) | Lesson details: (topic/objectives) LITERACY. Narratives. Learning objective – to write opposite character |
| Class/Year: 5 | TA: T. Allen (TA) | descriptions (i.e. Dracula and victim; superhero and villain) |

Time (minutes)	Lesson part *	With pupil one-to-one	With group of pupils	Roving classroom	Listening to teacher teach	Other task (tidying/admin)	TA-supported pupil(s) (name, attainment level, SEN status)	Task differentiation for TA-supported pupils	Comments on teacher's role	Features of TA-to-pupil talk
1	1				✓		TA sat on carpet with J (School Action +) & B (statement for MLD)		RL sets talk partner starter activity: words to describe your partner's appearance	Prompts to focus attention (pre-emptive)
2	1				✓					
3	1				✓					
4	1				✓					
5	1				✓					
6	1		✓				TA works with J & B for starter activity		RL observes class as they do talk partner task	Lots of TA talk. Little chance for J & B to interact with each other
7	1		✓							
8	1		✓							
9	1				✓		TA sat with J & B		RL gives whole class input	TA repeating RL's talk to J & B – questions, key words
10	1				✓					
11	1				✓					
12	1				✓					Prompt B to put up hand to answer RL's question
13	1				✓					
14	1				✓					
15	1				✓					
16	1				✓					Mostly passive; not interacting with pupils
17	1				✓					
18	1				✓					

Time (minutes)	Lesson part*	Predominant activity of TA					TA-supported pupil(s) (name, attainment level, SEN status)	Task differentiation for TA-supported pupils	Comments on teacher's role	Features of TA-to-pupil talk
		With pupil one-to-one	With group of pupils	Roving classroom	Listening to teacher teach	Other task (tidying/admin)				
19	T		✓				TA works with 4 lower-attaining pupils on Red table: J, B, C & D. TA sits next to B	RL tells TA that pupils on Red table need only describe one character – Dracula.	RL works with 5 higher-attaining pupils (5 mins). Use of high order questioning.	Clear explanation of task. Gives examples of adjectives. Checks understanding: "What are adjectives?"
20	T		✓							
21	T		✓							
22	T		✓							
23	T		✓						RL roves class, checks pupils are on-task & progressing. Roves to all tables but Red table	Some open questions used, not well targeted.
24	T		✓							
25	T		✓							Procedural talk: tells pupils to underline title, write date, make a start.
26	T		✓							
27	T		✓							
28	T		✓							
29	T			✓			As pupils begin task, TA withdraws from Red table. Roves between 2 average-attaining tables	Average-attaining pupils have to describe 2 characters	RL working with pair of pupils on average-attaining table	Promotes independence when asked for a spelling: "How can you find out for yourself?"
30	T			✓						
31	T			✓						
32	T			✓						
33	T				✓				RL talks to class to restate instructions	
34	T				✓					
35	T				✓					
36	T		✓				TA at Red table, checking progress. Pupils make slow start		RL uses laptop (3 mins)	Task-related: 'Come on. We need to get this done!', etc.
37	T		✓							
38	T		✓							

Table 2.7 continued

Time (minutes)	Lesson part *	With pupil one-to-one	With group of pupils	Roving classroom	Listening to teacher teach	Other task (tidying/admin)	TA-supported pupil(s) (name, attainment level, SEN status)	Task differentiation for TA-supported pupils	Comments on teacher's role	Features of TA-to-pupil talk
		Predominant activity of TA								
39	T	✓					TA gives one-to-one support to B who is off-task/disengaged		RL with average-attaining pupils. Evaluative questions: 'How would you feel if you met this scary character?'	TA repeats lots of closed questions. Little thinking time given for B to respond.
40	T	✓								
41	T	✓								
42	T	✓								
43	T	✓								
44	T	✓								
45	T		✓				TA draws J into interaction as he is having similar problem understanding abstract concept		RL at higher-attaining table: marking work, giving feedback	TA uses leading statements. Some spoon-feeding: 'We could say that Dracula has a long black cloak.'
46	T		✓							
47	T		✓							
48	T		✓							TA talks to RL.
49	T		✓							
50	T					✓				
51	T		✓				Supporting J & B		RL at Red table. Asks C and D to read their sentences out to her. Praises efforts	Task-related talk. TA seems keen that J & B have written something before end of lesson
52	T		✓							
53	T		✓							
54	P		✓							
55	P		✓							
56	P					✓	Collects in pupils' books		RL brings task to a close	
57	P					✓				
58	P				✓		Listens in to RL's plenary		RL leads plenary	
59	P				✓					
60	P				✓					
Total ✓		6	26	4	21	3				
Summary		10 %	43 %	7 %	35 %	5 %				

* Key for Lesson part: I = Teacher's main input T = Main learning task P = Plenary

The practice of TAs

A fine-grained description of TA-pupil interaction gets to the heart of what is central to all learning. Much of what TAs do in school involves working with pupils, yet we have found that these important interactions represent a 'black box', the lid of which is rarely, if ever, lifted. This is not to suggest that TA-pupil interactions are secretive, but merely to draw attention to a feature of classroom life that has long been taken for granted as well as overlooked. Given the centrality of interactions to learning outcomes, your audit should aim to provide a better understanding of the nature of TA-to-pupil talk, and the ways in which these interactions reflect the wider deployment and preparedness decisions that govern TAs' work.

For the purposes of the DISS project, we conducted a rigorous analysis of TA-to-pupil (and teacher-to-pupil) dialogue from transcriptions of recordings (Radford *et al.* 2012). The findings were extremely revealing, but this level of analysis may well be impractical for a school-based TA audit. An analysis of TA-pupil interactions adds a rich layer of detail that can often go undetected in an observation (e.g. because the observer is positioned too far away from the TA, or there is interference from general classroom noise).

An audit of TA-pupil talk can be nested within (that is, form part of) the classroom observations described above. The observation schedule (Table 2.7) has space in which you can write notes about TA-to-pupil talk in situ. But even better than this, in our view, is to make notes based on recordings of TA talk made during lessons, which can be played back as many times as you need. In the DISS project, we successfully used a digital voice recorder to capture TA talk unobtrusively.[5] The vast majority of TAs, who were often (and understandably) tentative about being recorded at first, told us afterwards that they quickly forgot about the recorder and spoke and acted as they would have had they not been wearing it. Nevertheless, as previously mentioned, you must be sensitive to the concerns of TAs who may feel 'over-scrutinised'. We cannot overstate the need for reassurance and transparency in the conduct of the audit.

Features of TA-to-pupil talk

The skilled and experienced practitioner will already know the features and purposes of classroom talk (e.g. prompting, questioning and so on), but we have drawn on our research and the literature on effective teaching to provide a directory of the common features of TA talk. This directory, shown in Table 2.8, provides descriptions and examples of the types of talk to which we recommend you are attentive, not least because some of these types of talk have been shown through our research to be less effective than others, in terms of their influence on pupil outcomes.

The directory should be considered indicative, rather than definitive; there may well be features you wish to add. Also, we do not mean to imply that certain types of talk are always ineffective; for example, there are occasions when asking a lower-order question is entirely appropriate if the aim is to elicit simple recall. The purpose of setting out the examples in Table 2.8 is to draw your attention to the fact that advancing pupil learning is impeded by the overuse of less effective types of talk. Our research shows that TAs tend not to take the opportunities in their interactions with pupils to ask higher-order questions, and this is principally because they are unaware of how to make use of the cues that invite such talk. TAs' routine use of spoon-feeding and leading statements, rather than encouraging pupils to think for themselves, encourages dependency.

Additionally, there are overarching features of talk, such as how TAs pace their talk and how they handle pupil responses that you should also wish to consider; for example, are pupils given adequate time to respond to a question?

In line with our advice on observations, you should pay attention to TA talk in relation to instances where TAs lead classes and where they deliver intervention sessions away from the classroom.

Table 2.8 Features of TA-to-pupil talk with examples

1. Closing down pupil talk	
Spoon-feeding (supplying answers)	The answer is a thousand.
Leading statements	The answer starts with a 'th' ... 'thou' ... 'thousan' ...
Lower-order/closed questions	Which of these shapes is a square? Who wrote this book?
2. Prioritising task completion	
Statements/prompts emphasising the need to complete the task	We've got to get this done by the end of the lesson. Come on. There's only five minutes of the lesson left before break.
3. Opening up pupil talk	
Statements to motivate; promote cognitive focus/engagement with task	You need to think about the words that you can use in your story. They need to be creative words that make up layers of meaning.
Higher-order/open questions	Can you tell me why that shape is called a square and why that shape is called a rectangle? How are you going to solve this problem? Where do we start when we see this kind of sum? Have you seen one before?
Probing a pupil's response	What do you mean when you describe the prince as 'posh'?
4. Providing explanations (with clarity and accuracy)	
Explaining a process	To divide 108 by 6, first note that 6 times 10 equals 60. So you subtract 60 from 108 and are left with 48. Then you tackle the smaller problem of 48 divided by 6.
Explaining a concept	The water cycle involves the sun heating the Earth's surface water and causing the surface water to evaporate.
Explaining an instruction	We have to put one spatula of copper sulphate in the beaker and then measure the temperature.
5. Drawing on prior learning	
Linking content of the current lesson to prior learning (e.g. from a previous lesson)	To help you, think about what we did last lesson when we were drawing two-dimensional shapes. What did we say 25% was equivalent to yesterday when we did fractions?
6. Managing pupil behaviour	
Reacting to off-task behaviour (e.g. reprimands)	If you are doodling, you're not listening. That tells me you're not doing the right thing.
Pre-emptive statements to prevent the likelihood of off-task behaviour	Put that away please. Why don't you come and sit here, so you're not tempted to mess about.
Focusing pupil attention	If you keep being good, I'll give you a sticker. Are you listening to the teacher? Face the board.

Case study

TAs observed by a teacher

Given the sizable task of addressing TA deployment at the school level, one secondary SENCo saw feedback on observations of TAs in action as one way of making some quick wins to avoid the negative effects of less effective types of TA practice. Drawing on the DISS project results, the SENCo developed a list of 'pitfalls' he noticed TAs unintentionally fell into in their interactions with pupils. These included: *'separation from classmates; unnecessary dependence; interference with teacher engagement; loss of personal control and provocation of poor behaviour.'* 'Things,' he said, *'that we could change very quickly in the way we approach things [and] avoid those pitfalls.'*

Preparedness of TAs (and teachers)

The final area your audit should cover is that of preparedness: the training received by TAs and teachers, and TAs' day-to-day preparation. Surveying the preparedness of your staff will help ascertain the extent to which TAs are briefed and made aware of their role in lessons, and how well equipped they are to carry out what is asked of them by teachers.

Training

Depending on how well informed you already are, it is also worth collecting data on TAs' training and qualifications, in order to build a complete picture of the courses they have completed and particular areas of knowledge and skills they possess. Given the wide variation in training routes and high number of courses available to TAs, we have found that the most effective method of collecting these data is to ask TAs in the form of an open-ended survey questionnaire, for information such as:

- *List any professional qualifications and training received relating to your role. (e.g. HLTA status, Foundation degree, NVQ in Supporting Teaching and Learning, the Support Work in Schools (SWiS) qualification, school-based Inset, mentoring training, training courses for SEN, training to deliver specific interventions, on-the-job training).*

In our experience, preparedness can be a sensitive area of enquiry, and so we recommend collecting the data on day-to-day preparation anonymously, via questionnaires (we will say more on this). However, as data on TAs' training and qualifications is less sensitive than this, in order to avoid the risk of compromising TAs' anonymity, we advise collecting this information separately. Asking the TAs to provide their names is necessary, as you will want to know your TAs' individual skills set.

As a result of this process, it may become immediately clear that certain individual TAs are inadequately prepared for teaching particular subjects, which will inform your decision-making about the appropriateness of the roles and demands of certain TAs and what you do about it (e.g. up-skilling or redeployment).

Day-to-day preparation

In terms of TAs' day-to-day preparation, the best people to ask, of course, are TAs. However, we have found through our own research that obtaining teachers' perceptions of TA preparedness is also very valuable. To this end, you should consider giving teachers and TAs the same questionnaire survey so that you can compare the responses between the two groups, exposing any differences or similarities in their perceptions.

We recommend that your survey of preparedness pays particular attention to gathering data on:

- The extent to which teachers and TAs have the opportunity for communication before lessons and for feedback afterwards
- The nature of teacher-TA communication, in terms of the level and quality of detail shared
- TAs' preparation for and feedback on intervention sessions, and the extent of teacher involvement
- How TAs acquire subject and instructional (pedagogical) knowledge.

To this end, we provide in Tables 2.9 to 2.16 examples of eight survey questions addressing these aspects of TA preparation, amended from versions used in the EDTA project audit. We have collated these questions in a photocopiable pro forma in Appendix 1. A blank version can be downloaded from our website.

These questions can be put to both teachers and TAs. Both groups should tick the statement that best matches their own experience. Each set of statements is ordered with what we would regard as the least effective practice at the top, and the most effective practice at the bottom. We acknowledge that the statements reflect broad circumstances and that the actual situation experienced by individuals is likely to be more complex than those described in the scenarios. Therefore, respondents should aim for the 'best fit'.

PRE-LESSON PREPARATION

When considering the effectiveness of your TAs, you will want to know the extent to which they have adequate opportunities to meet with teachers prior to lessons, and to plan, find out about and discuss the lesson and the role of the TA in it. In the DISS project, we found that 75% of teachers overall – and 95% in secondary schools – had no allocated time to meet with TAs, and that time to meet was dependent on TAs' goodwill. The example question in Table 2.9 is designed to help you ascertain the general experiences in your school.

Table 2.9 Example of survey question on pre-lesson preparedness 1

Opportunity for teacher-TA pre-lesson communication	✓
1) No opportunity/time to communicate before lessons	
2) Communication before lessons is brief and ad hoc	
3) TA comes in early/stays behind after school to meet with teacher for briefing	
4) Teacher and TA have scheduled time to meet (e.g. time for which TA is paid)	

Some TAs and teachers have or create time to meet; others do not. In this case, written forms of pre-lesson communication are necessary in order for teachers to impart to TAs information about lessons and what role they want them to play in them. In the DISS project, we found that TAs received little or no pre-lesson information via lesson plans. Some teachers use either their lesson plan or a teacher-TA communication book to impart information, but the quality varied. We used the question in Table 2.10 in the EDTA project to collect baseline data on this aspect of preparedness.

Table 2.10 Example of survey question on pre-lesson preparedness 2

Quality of preparation for TA (teachers' lesson plans)	✓
1) TA goes into lessons blind. No lesson plan provided	
2) TA given lesson plan. No specific information about TA role given	
3) TA given lesson plan. Limited information about TA role given (e.g. names of pupils to support)	
4) TA given lesson plan. Specific information about TA role given (e.g. specific objectives/ outcomes)	

POST-LESSON FEEDBACK

Again, in the DISS project, we found around three-quarters of teachers had no allocated time to meet with TAs for feedback. As a result, the quality of feedback was at a general and basic level, and had little value in terms of informing teachers' subsequent lesson planning. The example questions in Tables 2.11 and 2.12 mirror the two questions above, reflecting the opportunity for and quality of feedback after lessons.

Table 2.11 Example of survey question on post-lesson feedback 1

Opportunity for teacher-TA post-lesson communication	✓
1) No opportunity/time to communicate after lessons	
2) Communication after lessons is brief and ad hoc	
3) TA comes in early/stays behind after school to meet with teacher for debriefing	
4) Teacher and TA have scheduled time to meet (e.g. time for which TA is paid)	

Table 2.12 Example of survey question on post-lesson feedback 2

Quality of TA feedback to teachers (written/verbal)	✓
1) TA does not feed information back to teachers	
2) TA feeds back basic information (e.g. 'task completed'; 'pupils on-task')	
3) TA feeds back detailed information (e.g. specific problems with/progress towards learning goals)	

INTERVENTIONS

One aspect of our research observed in both the DISS and EDTA studies was the extent to which TAs had taken on the responsibility for planning and delivering interventions and booster sessions (usually away from the classroom). Other research on the use of TAs to deliver intervention projects (e.g. by Alborz *et al.* 2009) is clear on the positive impact this can have on pupil attainment, although caveats are often made that success is only likely to follow if TAs are properly prepared and supported in this role.

Furthermore, it should also be possible to judge the effects of any intervention in terms of evidence of progress in pupils' wider learning. This, we argue, is only possible when teachers and TAs bridge learning across the two contexts of the classroom and the intervention space (e.g. outside the classroom). To do that, an effective process of preparation and feedback needs to be in place. The example questions in Tables 2.13 and 2.14 will help you derive the extent to which this could be the case in your school.

Such questions will help you to obtain a sense of how well interventions are integrated into mainstream learning in the classroom. One further question you should ask in your audit is to what extent the targets set for individual pupils in relation to interventions match their National Curriculum targets set by the class teacher (see Chapter 3).

Table 2.13 Example of survey question on interventions 1

Preparation for interventions: guidance from teachers	✓
1) TA plans and prepares interventions, with very little/no input from teachers	
2) TA plans and prepares interventions, with some general guidance from teachers	
3) TA plans and prepares interventions, with substantive, detailed guidance from teachers	

Table 2.14 Example of survey question on interventions 2

Feedback on interventions: quality of TA's feedback to teachers (written/verbal)	✓
1) TA does not feed information back to teachers	
2) TA feeds back basic information (e.g. 'task completed'; 'pupils on-task')	
3) TA feeds back detailed information (e.g. specific problems with/progress towards learning goals)	

TAs' SUBJECT AND INSTRUCTIONAL KNOWLEDGE

TAs do not have the same level of training as teachers, and the majority are not graduates in a particular subject or discipline as teachers are. Plus, we know from the DISS project that teachers and TAs have little time in which to communicate. So this begs a question: how do TAs acquire the subject and instructional knowledge necessary for them to do their job?

The example questions in Tables 2.15 and 2.16 will help you to obtain an understanding of how TAs obtain essential knowledge: from, at one level, picking it up as the teacher delivers it to the class, through the familiar means of ad hoc communication, to – at the more effective end – more robust methods of full briefings and training.

Table 2.15 Example of survey question on TAs' subject knowledge

6.1 Subject knowledge	✓
1) TA gains subject knowledge by tuning in to teacher delivery (e.g. as part of class audience)	
2) TA gains subject knowledge from lesson plans and/or schemes of work	
3) TA gains subject knowledge via ad hoc communication with teacher	
4) TA gains subject knowledge via substantive briefing/training from teacher	
5) TA has significant level of subject knowledge via specific training (e.g. TA has degree in subject)	

Table 2.16 Example of survey question on TAs' instructional knowledge

6.2 *Instructional knowledge*	✓
1) TA gains instructional knowledge by tuning in to teacher delivery (e.g. as part of class audience)	
2) TA gains instructional knowledge from lesson plans and/or schemes of work	
3) TA gains instructional knowledge via ad hoc communication with teacher	
4) TA gains instructional knowledge via substantive briefing/training from teacher	
5) TA has significant level of instructional knowledge via specific training (e.g. TA has QTS)	

You may wish to ask additional questions about the specific knowledge TAs may possess in terms of curriculum coverage; that is, facts, concepts and processes related to a particular subject. This will vary across subjects and so the formulation of the questions should involve teachers, since they are best placed to identify and determine a 'minimum threshold' of such knowledge.

Other audit questions you should consider

TEACHERS' PREPAREDNESS TO WORK WITH AND MANAGE TAs

As we argued earlier, your teachers may also be inadequately prepared to work with and manage TAs. Therefore, it is important for you to discover the extent to which teachers feel prepared or adequately trained to work with and manage TAs. One way of obtaining this information would be to give teachers additional survey questions on this topic. Another method would be to use the teacher focus group, mentioned earlier in this chapter, as a forum for exploring this issue.

TEACHERS' KNOWLEDGE OF SEN

Another element of preparedness very much bound up with TAs' preparedness for the roles and tasks given to them by teachers, concerns teachers' knowledge of SEN. This includes the identification and understanding of the most common types of SEN and the knowledge of, and skill in, using pedagogic strategies suited to pupils with those needs. The audit should be used to elicit this information. You may find, in line with the DISS project findings, that a very patchy picture will emerge, with some teachers having more or less – or even no – suitable preparation to teach pupils with SEN. If you find that this patchy picture applies to your school, you will be compelled to do something about it, and the audit will provide you with a starting point from which to proceed.

PERFORMANCE MANAGEMENT FOR TAs

There are structured annual performance management procedures in place for teachers, but many schools do not have as rigorous a process in place for TAs. As a result of reforming the way in which TAs are deployed and prepared in your school, we would expect you to address this and put in place a process to review TA performance and identify any training needs. A necessary component of your audit will therefore be to consider what performance review processes you already have in place – formal and informal – and consider how these could be made more systematic, rigorous and relevant to their specific individual role.

PUPIL VOICE

We have chosen not to include input from pupils in our recommendations concerning the audit. However, you may feel that it is important to seek their opinions as part of your review of current practice, or indeed consult them on proposed changes to TA deployment. Furthermore, you may wish to involve parents, particularly those of pupils with SEN, who are likely to be most affected by changes to the existing practice. Alison Ekins' book, *The Changing Face of Special Educational Needs* (2012), contains helpful suggestions on consulting pupils and parents.

Summary

The aim of this chapter has been to build on the questions raised in the book so far, and to provide you with the tools to conduct an audit of current practice. Any process of change in any organisation must begin from a position of clarity in terms of how things are presently. In other words, you need to know what to change and the extent of change needed before you can enact it. This will ensure that resources are targeted effectively and the whole process is efficient.

Finally, once the process is set up, the auditing tools can be used again at a later date to help you evaluate the extent of change; essentially providing you with an 'after' picture to set alongside the 'before' picture. We recommend that you perform some form of evaluation (e.g. an observation) at regular intervals, so that any changes that are not effective can be altered. We summarise the key questions your audit should address:

- *What proportion of time do TAs spend on teaching and learning activities, and other tasks?*
- *What roles do teachers and TAs have in classrooms? Which pupils do they spend most time with, and in which contexts (e.g. groups)?*
- *What is the purpose of TAs in your school? How is the TA role distinct from the role of teachers?*
- *What roles do TAs have when working away from the classroom? Which pupils do they spend most time with, and in which contexts?*
- *How is differentiation handled for pupils with SEN?*
- *What are the characteristics of TAs' talk to pupils?*
- *How well prepared are teachers for working with and managing TAs?*
- *What is the level and quality of TA preparation? To what extent is this helped or impeded by the opportunity for teacher-TA communication?*
- *What is the level and quality of TAs' preparation for intervention sessions and the extent of teacher involvement?*

Chapter 3

The deployment of TAs

Introduction

The DISS project findings made it clear that there are aspects of the deployment of TAs that need to be changed in order to avoid the damaging effects that their support can have on pupils' academic progress. As described in the Introduction, we have set out the main body of this book using the structure of the Wider Pedagogical Role (WPR) model, and for each of the three main components we cover (deployment, practice and preparedness), we address decision-making at the school level and the classroom level.

It is likely that as you read through this chapter on TA deployment you will consider the need to prepare TAs properly for their roles, in the form of training and providing opportunities for teachers and TAs to meet throughout the week. As will already be clear, we wholeheartedly agree that adequate preparation is essential if you are to get the best out of your TAs, and we have particular recommendations about training and creating time for planning and feedback time for teachers and TAs in Chapter 4. However, we have avoided making too much of this in this section in order to concentrate on the starting point from which all other decisions about TAs flow. This chapter asks you to consider the following question: what is the role and purpose of TAs in your school, and how should they be deployed?

Reviewing and defining the role of the TA: school-level decisions

The findings from the DISS project prompt a fundamental question that school leaders *must* address: given that we found TAs at present have an ineffective instructional role, should they have a pedagogical role at all? Should they teach pupils directly?

If the answer is yes – and most schools we have worked with have taken this route – we need to work out what this pedagogical role should be. If, on the other hand, we take the view that TAs should not have a pedagogical role, then we must again decide what this non-pedagogical role should be. It is our view that this issue has been given far too little attention, even though it is at the heart of many other issues connected to the use of TAs. Both views are defensible, but both require careful consideration of the consequences. Throughout this chapter, we raise some important questions you will need to consider when assigning broadly pedagogical and non-pedagogical roles to individual TAs.

The process of review and redefinition of TAs' roles across the school must be initiated by the SLT, but it is essential that teachers and TAs are involved early on in the series of changes that you can expect to flow from it.

The audit process set out in the previous chapter allows you to review the present deployment of TAs in your school, and it will reveal the extent to which your TAs teach pupils, both in and away from the classroom. It will also identify the non-pedagogical roles that they have (e.g. doing admin tasks for teachers). A school-wide consultation of all TAs, surveying them about their perception of their role can prove to be very revealing; there may be a wide variation in perceptions. The findings from such consultations can be used to inform the development of a school policy on TA deployment. Once you have this information, you will be in the position to make decisions about formally defining the TAs' roles across the school.

It may be thought best to combine elements of a pedagogical and a non-pedagogical role for some or all of your TAs. This will be informed by what you find in your audit of TAs' individual strengths and skills sets; some TAs will be more appropriately deployed in teaching roles than others if, for example, their subject knowledge is particularly strong. This would be a school-level choice, setting the boundaries for deployment decisions at the class level made by individual teachers.

Key recommendations on reviewing the present deployment of TAs

- Conduct a school-wide audit in order to establish the need for change and the extent of change required (see Chapter 2). Ensure that good practice is identified and built upon.
- Ensure that significant changes to models of TA deployment are supported by adequate training and guidance (see Chapter 4).

Non-pedagogical and pedagogical roles for TAs

We will spend the rest of this section on school-level deployment decisions, exploring the various options and decisions that arise from your decision to deploy TAs in non-pedagogical and pedagogical roles. We will explore each in turn in more detail, after we have offered some guidance on deciding your staffing structure. Before we do, however, it is worth setting out briefly what we mean by non-pedagogical and pedagogical TA roles.

A non-pedagogical role for TAs

If you choose to replace TAs' direct teaching role with a non-teaching role, you will need to define their new role and identify the tasks that you feel contribute to the effectiveness of the teachers and the school. The research evidence suggests three main non-pedagogical roles that TAs can adopt, and which can lead to positive outcomes (see Blatchford, Russell and Webster 2012):

1 Supporting the teacher, in terms of carrying out routine tasks such as preparing and organising materials
2 Helping with classroom organisation and ensuring lessons run more smoothly by encouraging pupils to focus on tasks and 'nipping in the bud' any off-task or disruptive behaviour
3 Providing direct support for pupils with physical and emotional needs, both in class and in the wider context of the school.

In this section, we will additionally flag the potential for TAs to take on a form of parent liaison role. The importance and value of such a role, acting as a trusted mediator between school and home, is gaining prominence, as greater emphasis is placed on parental engagement in pupils' learning and school life in general.

As a school leader, you must give thought to the optimum balance of direct and indirect forms of TA support for pupils and teachers (e.g. performing tasks that require and do not require a high degree of interaction with pupils) and the possibility of developing a variety of TA roles. We will return to this point.

If you decide to limit the role of some or all of your TAs to non-pedagogical roles, the implementation will expose the need for changes in TAs' preparation and training for these newly configured roles. Day-to-day preparation for their work will also become a clearer issue and steps will be needed to make this effective (see Chapter 4).

A pedagogical role for TAs

The audit process will reveal the extent and form of the TAs' present pedagogical role. If you recognised many of the issues highlighted in our earlier presentation of the findings from the DISS project, it is likely that the TAs in your school have a considerable teaching role, which may be more substantive than you initially imagined.

The complete picture provided by the audit will raise questions about the TAs' role both in classrooms alongside teachers and away from classrooms and teachers. The DISS project findings challenge you to review the present deployment of TAs in a pedagogical role in these two contexts and to make changes where they are required.

If you choose to retain a role for TAs in which they have an interactive role with pupils, the school needs to agree the details of what this should involve, and express it formally in the shape of a school policy on TA deployment. We have found that the vast majority of schools have no such policy and the situation on the ground is often very ad hoc and subject to enormous variation across classes, as individual teachers have been left to make deployment decisions. Leadership decisions of the sort we are advocating, aimed at achieving coordination and consistency across the school, have rarely been made.

Some important questions to ask about the pedagogical role of TAs

- Is it reasonable to expect TAs to be as effective as teachers when teaching pupils, given that they do not have the same levels of training?
- Where is the appropriate boundary between the teaching roles of teachers and TAs?
- What is the limit, in terms of responsibility and accountability to parents and the school governing body, of TAs who teach?
- What does 'working under the supervision of the teacher' actually mean and look like in your school?
- Should teachers delegate the teaching of pupils with the most demanding learning needs to TAs, who are generally without relevant professional qualifications?
- Are TAs who teach given the status, professional development opportunities, participation in decision-making about teaching and learning, and salaries that reflect these responsibilities?

These are the 'hard' questions that must be addressed when opting to deploy TAs in a pedagogical role. The DISS project has shown that many such questions have not been addressed at the school level, resulting in many forms of ineffective practice and damage being done to pupils' progress, in particular those who are most disadvantaged. Individual teachers have been left to make these deployment decisions – with little if any training or guidance to inform them – and have seldom been asked to justify their choices or evaluate their effectiveness.

As with the development of the non-pedagogical role outlined above, the process leading to clearly defined pedagogical roles will need to be handled in ways that include teachers, TAs, SLT and, maybe, external agencies. It will need to start from a fully informed position via the audit, and the issue of the appropriate level for particular deployment choices – school or classroom – will have to be addressed. Answering this question will clarify what the policy will need to cover in detail and will provide a framework within which individual teachers can operate, making it clearer which decisions are permissible when deploying TAs to teach pupils, in or out of the classroom.

Drawing up a school policy on TA deployment

Teachers and TAs will need to have clear guidelines to enable them all to conform to the redefined TA roles and the simplest way to provide such guidance is to develop a school policy on TA deployment. Through the process of its development and its implementation, the boundaries between the roles of teachers and TAs will be discussed and clarified, and a shared understanding will be established, in terms of how the pedagogical and non-pedagogical roles of TAs can be managed by teachers to maximise the benefits of TAs at the classroom level.

Pupils will also need to be made aware of the ways in which the school will deploy TAs, since many have become over-dependent on them. All teachers will need to explain to their pupils the new forms of teamwork that they have agreed to introduce in their classes and which require deploying TAs in ways that depart from previous practice.

The parents of pupils with statements of SEN should also be included in this information sharing exercise, as the benefits of new, modified or different models of TA deployment will need to be explained to parents who have become familiar with – or expect – particular models of TA usage.

Such major changes will present challenges to everyone within the school; they will not be fully operational immediately and there are bound to be periods of adjustment along the way as new forms of practice become embedded. The more thorough and open the processes of consultation, data collection, decision-making, dissemination and implementation, the faster and more smoothly the road to more effective ways of deploying your TAs will be.

Key recommendations on the school policy on TA deployment

- Recognise the importance of clarifying the pedagogical role of TAs relative to teachers.
- With your SLT, address the hard questions suggested above, and use the answers to frame your philosophy about TA deployment.
- Draft a policy on TA deployment, setting out a framework within which teachers will have some flexibility at classroom level. Be clear about how class teachers will be able to deploy TAs and what is no longer permissible.

Clarifying the role of each TA

Decisions about staffing structure

With your policy in the advanced stages of development, you will want to address the issue of clarifying the role each of your TAs will take on. The DISS project has shown very clearly that more deliberate and conscious choices need to be made regarding the deployment of TAs, moving away from the routine, default position of deploying all TAs on the same basis in a generic role, to a more purposeful and methodical alignment of specific roles and individuals.

We will address specific points you will need to consider when assigning non-pedagogical and pedagogical roles to individual TAs, but first we set out the two main ways in which you and your SLT approach these decisions about determining your staffing structure.

The blank page approach

The first approach is what we might call the 'blank page' approach. This method assumes you are starting from scratch, as if you do not have any TAs in your school at present. You then decide the TA staffing structure you want in terms of the broad roles you require. Questions you need to ask will include:

- *How many TAs do you want to have a wholly pedagogical role, and to which year groups would they be assigned?*
- *Do you require a TA or TAs in pedagogical roles to provide cover for teachers when they take their PPA time?*
- *How many 'classroom helpers' do you want (e.g. TAs with a non-pedagogical role who can assist teachers with routine tasks in the classroom)?*
- *How many TAs are needed to support pupils with physical mobility needs?*
- *How many TAs do you require in a nurturing capacity (e.g. Emotional Literacy Support Assistants)?*

Here we couch the questions in terms of personnel, assuming that these TA roles are full-time posts, but of course, there are other ways in which these questions can be presented; for example, in terms of how many hours of TA time are required for PPA cover, supporting physical needs, etc. However, we note that there will be implications for pay if, for example, you deploy a HLTA as a classroom helper for part of the week; the use of 'split contracts' (e.g. paying TAs at different rates depending on the tasks they do) is not in line with the aims of workforce reform and the principles of the National Agreement (WAMG 2008).

Some schools we know of have found it helpful to use national standards for obtaining HLTA status and TA role profiles produced by their local authority, which outline the key responsibilities and entry level requirements for TAs at several graded levels, to help make these decisions about staffing. Using the blank page approach, you will be able to establish a set of TA roles, which are distinct from one another and from the role of teachers.

The next step is to map your existing TAs on to the roles you identified in the above exercise, using the details from your audit of TAs' skills and qualifications. Some TAs have strengths in providing warmth, empathy and encouragement, and have a firm but sensitive authority, which would make them suited to working with pupils in nurturing roles. Other

TAs may have a degree in a particular subject specialism and would be suitably deployed to support lessons in that subject.

The key principle is to develop roles more consciously and purposefully, and to ensure and specify the minimum level of expertise expected for each role. Every effort must be made to avoid defaulting to the current and widespread – and ineffective – forms of TA deployment, which do not vary across year groups, classes, subjects or the individuals who occupy these roles.

There may be roles that are not filled by individuals, and, conversely, TAs who do not have roles within your new structure. However, this process will highlight training needs for specific individuals, who can be trained to meet the role requirements.

The retrofit approach

We call the second approach to deciding your staffing structure the 'retrofit' approach, meaning that the process described above is essentially reversed. You begin the retrofit approach by examining the TA skills set audit, and then base your staffing structure on these results. In other words, you work with what you have in order to redesign the existing structure. However, it is important to note that this approach will not necessarily give schools the TA staffing structure they *need* or that aligns with an ideal model.

The retrofit approach involves first confirming the levels at which your TAs are working. Some schools have found it useful to carry out this exercise with recourse to the aforementioned TA role profiles or other similar frameworks, as it helps ascertain the degree to which TAs are working within their current grading. It can also reveal whether TAs are being deployed to their maximum effect or whether there are any TAs who are being stretched (perhaps unfairly) beyond their current capabilities and level of training.

Once you feel you know your TAs well enough, you can select the criteria on which you will base their position within your structure. Their qualifications, specialisms, strengths, experience of particular year groups, subjects and partnerships with teachers, may all figure in your decisions. As with the blank page method, training needs will be readily identifiable via this approach.

Consultation

We note that changing your TA staffing structure may involve wider consultations as changes to contracts and conditions of employment have legal ramifications. Many local authorities will have a policy and adviser on staff restructuring, which maintained schools will be able to consult. Schools that fall outside local authority control (e.g. academies) may have to consult their own advisers on employment law. It may also be necessary to consult with local union representatives (e.g. Unison).

At the school level, school leaders may not be able to implement changes without approval from the governing body. Governors are often consulted on developments that have financial implications for the school. On this issue, it is worth noting that restricting your TA workforce may incur some costs upfront, but we know of no legal bar to the kind of fundamental restructuring we are advocating in this book.

Key recommendations on clarifying the role of each TA

- Conduct a survey of TAs' skills, qualifications and training received as part of your school audit.
- Review the current TA roles and consider having a variety of distinct roles within a new TA staffing structure (e.g. direct pupil support (including for interventions) roles, teacher/classroom support roles, subject-specific roles, and nurturing and care roles.
- Conduct appropriate consultations with legal and union representatives, and the school's governing body.

Defining the non-pedagogical role for TAs

As we have described, the overtly non-pedagogical roles that TAs can have are broadly concerned with assisting teachers with routine tasks and classroom behaviour, and having a nurturing or welfare role, supporting pupils' physical and emotional needs. Here, we also consider a role for TAs in relation to parent liaison.

Supporting the work of teachers

Perhaps the most extreme expression of a non-pedagogical role is one that requires little, if any, interaction with pupils, and instead helps teachers with their routine clerical tasks, like photocopying. We know from the DISS project that such deployment of TAs and other support staff contributed to reducing teacher workloads and positively affected their job satisfaction (Blatchford, Russell and Webster 2012). We doubt many school leaders would be convinced that this model will be appropriate for their entire current TA workforce, but there may be a case for developing, say, one TA post for this type of work – undertaken largely away from the classroom. If so, you will need to define which tasks teachers can delegate to TAs.

The DISS project showed that one way TAs had benefits for teachers was in the classroom, in terms of classroom management. Ofsted (2005) have pointed out that the main behaviour problem in schools is the 'persistent, low-level disruption of lessons that wears down staff and disrupts learning'. The DISS project found that the presence of TAs limits the need for teachers to manage this kind of problem. You might consider developing an effective non-instructional role for TAs in which they act as an extra set of eyes and ears, noticing negative and off-task behaviour, and stepping in to address it without disrupting the teacher's delivery or flow of the lesson.

We note, however, that while Giangreco and Broer (2005) found that although TAs spent one-fifth of their time providing behavioural support to pupils, TAs were relatively untrained and underprepared, and often lacking in confidence when it came to managing pupils with challenging behaviour. If you develop such roles for TAs, it is imperative that those who occupy these roles are thoroughly trained in classroom management techniques and are recognised by staff and pupils as legitimate enforcers of the school's behaviour policy. Teachers, however, must have ultimate responsibility for the management of behaviour in the classroom; it is not a duty to be wholly delegated to TAs.

The limits of this role have to be made clear to teachers, in order to inform their classroom deployment decisions; they must be aware of what TAs would be expected and not expected to do in these roles. The appropriate use of TAs as classroom behaviour monitors must be covered in your school policy on TAs.

Supporting pupils' physical and emotional needs

Some TAs in some schools will already have a role connected to the support of pupils with physical needs of some kind (e.g. mobility, visual or hearing impairment). Many of these TAs require, and will have received, special training, in, for example, handling and physiotherapy techniques, sign language and in the use of special equipment. Such support from TAs is vital for those pupils who might otherwise have to attend a special school, not because of a learning need (some will not have any such difficulties), but because of the accessibility of buildings, equipment and the curriculum.

The issue for school leaders to consider is this: what proportion of the time do TAs in such roles *actually* spend supporting pupils' physical needs, and what proportion of the time do they do other things. While there is clear value in TAs performing roles that many teachers will not be able to do concurrent with leading the class (e.g. signing for hearing impaired pupils), the DISS project concurrently revealed the problems that occur when TAs with such responsibilities stray into or are expected to take on pedagogical functions for which they are far less prepared.

The audit will reveal whether there is capacity for TAs in such roles to perform other roles at times when they are not supporting pupils' physical needs. For example, if the supported pupil is able to work independently in a lesson, this creates an opportunity for them to assist the teacher or other pupils in another way (in either a pedagogical or non-pedagogical role). The point here is that if you decide to expand the role of these TAs, it must be clear to them and teachers what the extended limits of their new role are, and new responsibilities must be supported by training.

TA roles that support pupils' emotional needs are particularly well delineated, as they typically have less to do with the pedagogical role of teachers. TAs in these roles are likely to deliver specific programmes aimed at exploring and developing pupils' emotional literacy and coping skills.

This role is a different expression of the paraprofessional role. It is the role of other professionals (sometimes as part of a multi-disciplinary team) to deal with pupils' often complex problems. TAs, however, can provide invaluable support to these wider processes by helping pupils to share thoughts and feelings.

Results from the DISS project showed that teachers value the knowledge that TAs have of pupils because they worked so closely with them, and therefore heard about important things in their life that influenced their mood and wellbeing. Additionally, TAs often have knowledge about pupils based on the fact that they live in the same neighbourhood, unlike teachers, who are more likely to live out of the catchment area. Therefore, they can be more aware of how family and community life affect pupils.

Fraser and Meadows (2008) found that pupils characterised the best TAs as demonstrating care, kindliness, friendliness, helpfulness, warmth and attentiveness. Dunne *et al.* (2008) highlight TAs' functional priorities in terms of a predominantly nurturing role. Therefore, it is perhaps unsurprising that we found, in the DISS project, that interactions between TAs and pupils are often less formal and more intimate than those between teachers and pupils; pupils viewed TAs as being closer to 'their level' than teachers.

Many TAs, then, have the background and dispositions well suited to supporting pupils' pastoral needs, and you may choose to develop some specific non-pedagogical roles to capitalise on this. We are aware of a number of schools that are training TAs to become Emotional Literacy Support Assistants (ELSAs).[6] TAs qualify following a structured programme of training and supervision from educational psychologists. ELSAs plan and deliver individual and small group support programmes to help pupils with social and emotional difficulties to recognise, understand and manage their emotions, to increase their wellbeing and success in school. While such roles are underpinned by training and support, we argue that there are particular risks that can stem from TAs selecting, planning, delivering and assessing interventions with little input from teachers of which you need to be aware. We will deal with this issue in more detail.

Parent liaison

Parental support and engagement are critical factors in how well children achieve. Therefore, schools have long been concerned with the lack of engagement exhibited by some parents in their child's learning. In some cases, the lack of engagement can be explained by parents' own negative experiences of school and learning when they were growing up. Some parents develop a distrust of authority and distance themselves from schools and other social institutions.

Such attitudes are often exaggerated among parents of lower-income families. There are a higher proportion of pupils with SEN from lower-income families compared with those from middle- and higher-income families. Schools serving families in areas of deprivation often find it more difficult to engage with parents of the pupils who need the most support.

As we have mentioned, a school typically draws its TA workforce from the catchment area it serves. This, together with the personal qualities listed above, puts TAs in a strong position to act as effective mediators or 'connectors' between the school and parents.

We do not intend to provide any further guidance in this book on developing parent liaison or support roles for TAs. If this interests you, you might like to consider a home-liaison role (e.g. as a Parent Support Advisers or via the Portage scheme), a supporting (not a lead) role in structured conversations with parents[7] or family interventions, such as Family SEAL (social and emotional aspects of learning) or the Positive Parenting Programme. Your local authority will be able to advise you.

Key recommendations on defining the non-pedagogical roles of TAs

- Define the remit of non-pedagogical roles; for example, in terms of the routine tasks that TAs should and should not do; or the appropriate level of intervention in managing behaviour.
- Ensure that any role change or extension is supported by training and is consistent with school policy on, for example, interventions or behaviour management.

Defining the pedagogical role for TAs

The decision to deploy some or all of your TAs in a pedagogical role (in whole or in part) prompts a set of further issues you will need to address. Based on our research, there are some particular questions we suggest you, as a school leader, should ask when defining the composition and parameters of the pedagogical role of TAs. We summarise these below before exploring each one in turn:

1   *What role should TAs have as part of the school's provision for lower-attaining pupils and, in particular, those with SEN?*

2   *Do we want TAs to teach intervention programmes? If so, do we need to improve on the present model of deployment?*

3   *Do we want TAs to lead classes as part of the school's PPA and/or short-term teacher cover arrangements?*

4   *Should we change the allocation of TAs across classes, year groups and/or subjects? (A question particularly relevant to secondary school leaders)*

5   *Are changes needed to TAs' job specifications, conditions of employment and salaries? How will these changes affect TAs already in post and any future appointments?*

You may decide that some individual TAs should have greater pedagogical responsibilities than others; for example, given the present situation as revealed by the audit of TAs' skills, some might be more appropriately deployed to lead classes as part of PPA arrangements than others. In which case, you will need to ask the questions above with individual TAs in mind to determine the limitations of their pedagogical role. The questions above are useful for determining the outermost limits of the pedagogical role; in other words, just how far should the TAs' teaching role extend into the territory of the teachers' teaching role, given that we want to keep both distinct? Again, in our experience, this is an issue that schools rarely tackle, but on which all practitioners have a view.

TAs and pupils with SEN

The most serious questions raised by the DISS project findings concerned schools' provision for the education of pupils with SEN, both with and without statements. As we have explained, the damage done to their progress can be directly linked to the way TAs are deployed to teach them *in place of* teachers. The TA often becomes the adult from whom individual pupils receive the most attention and have the most interactions. If, in addition, the TA takes any such pupils out of the class to work on tasks that are different from those that the rest of the class are doing, there are further consequences in terms of separating the TA-supported pupils from the mainstream curriculum and their peers. As a result of these arrangements, such pupils, whose learning is already behind that of their peers, are likely to make even less progress. Again, the situation can be exacerbated if, as is very often the case, the class teacher fails to integrate the out-of-class teaching and learning with what happens in the classroom.

Changes you make will need to reverse this situation. *Teachers must become the adult with whom pupils with SEN have regular, sustained and focused interactions, and these pupils must remain part of the teaching and learning experience provided in the classroom as much as possible.*

Perhaps the clearest message from the DISS project is that TAs must not be routinely deployed to teach lower-attaining pupils and those with SEN. There will need to be a clear and firm message from you to teachers that such deployment practices are no longer adequate. You should make it clear that you will be looking for evidence of teachers taking responsibility for the teaching and learning of *all* pupils in the observations made as part of your monitoring process. In this sense, you are reinforcing what has, legally speaking, always been the case. Indeed, it is also what Ofsted inspectors with the responsibility for assessing SEN are also looking for (Ofsted 2011b).

Case study

Presence vs. impact: provision for pupils with SEN

In their considerations of alternative models of TA deployment (e.g. locating TAs within subject departments), schools in the EDTA project – and in particular, secondary schools – weighed up how they could implement these new models while retaining enough TA hours to meet the support needs of pupils with a statement for SEN. The need for continuity of support was seen as important for effective provision. TAs, therefore, remained inextricably linked with the provision for SEN, and it seemed that, in some cases, parental pressure might have been a driving factor in maintaining the deployment of TAs in this way.

One secondary school found that these parental expectations were heightened during the period of discussing transition from primary to secondary school. Parents of a pupil with a statement for SEN requested that their child received one-to-one support from a TA in secondary school, as he/she had in primary school. The SENCo, who was acutely aware of the negative impact that this form of TA deployment could have on pupil outcomes (as revealed through the DISS project), wanted to challenge the tendency for parents to expect, and even demand, that their child should have one-to-one TA support in circumstances where teachers could provide more effective input. Achieving this, the SENCo noted, would require an additional approach: challenging the typical '*discourse on using a teaching assistant, which is normally about presence rather than impact*'. The SENCo's starting point had been to remind teachers that they were responsible for the engagement and learning of all pupils in their classes. He wanted the school to move away from a culture of using TAs to 'tick the box for inclusion'.

'*[Teachers] feel like they can meet the needs of children with learning difficulties if there is another adult present. Not to do anything specifically, but simply to be there to have contact with that child. They feel like that ticks the box for meeting need; when we know that, not only is that not the case, but it can make things worse.*'

Later in this chapter, we set out how schools can open up the TA role in the classroom by making simple changes to deployment routines. But school leaders need to lead cultural change at the organisational level. Teachers must be encouraged to reconsider how they deploy TAs across attainment groups and how the school at large needs to abandon the 'Velcro TA' model, where pupils with statements are attached to a TA. Doing so, we argue, reduces pupil separation from the teacher, increases pupil independence and increases the amount of interaction teachers have with lower-attaining pupils and those with SEN.

Key recommendations on defining the pedagogical role of TAs

- Lead a whole-school drive to abandon ineffective models of TA deployment in relation to pupils with SEN.
- Ensure that this is a collaborative effort, and that teachers and TAs know that SLT will support them through the process of change.

- Work towards a situation where the pupils with the greatest level of need have *at least* the same amount of time with teachers as their peers.

TAs and intervention programmes

If TAs in your school are deployed to carry out intervention programmes (commonly for literacy and numeracy, but also for language) and you intend to continue this form of the pedagogical role, then you will need to review all aspects of your current arrangements.

In the DISS project, we found that in many cases, TAs were asked to select, prepare, teach and assess the learning outcomes of interventions, very often without any active involvement of the teachers responsible for the pupils. We argue that this practice is ineffective and can be both wasteful of the TAs' time and contribute to the separation of the pupils involved from the work and life of the class, and from interactions with their teachers. At worst, we have heard that this carousel of withdrawal for various interventions amounts to 'a lifestyle' for some pupils. Interventions are not a default substitute for quality first teaching.

We have found that teachers are very often unaware of what tasks are done in the intervention sessions, and are therefore unable to integrate or build on them in subsequent class sessions. Even when they *do* know the content of the tasks, they generally do not attempt to 'bridge across' from one part of the pupil's learning experience (outside the class) to the other (inside the class). It is left to the pupil him/herself themselves to see the links and apply the learning from one context in the other – a very demanding expectation. It is these signs of integration that Ofsted inspectors are looking for (Ofsted 2011b).

As a school, you need to review how intervention programmes are taught and how effective they are in fulfilling the overall learning needs of pupils.

Some important questions to ask about TAs and intervention programmes

- *Do we select interventions to use that have a sound evidence base and are proven to work?*
- *Are we using good programmes badly?*
- *What are the aims and objectives of each of our intervention programmes?*
- *Do we know how well we achieve these aims and objectives with individual pupils?*
- *How do we evaluate pupil progress and the effectiveness of interventions?*
- *Do we ever adjust or even close down any ineffective programmes?*
- *Will TAs be asked to prepare the intervention sessions without input from the teachers of the pupils involved? If so, how do we justify this arrangement and ensure that teachers are aware of the tasks and learning objectives of the intervention sessions?*
- *Will interventions be carried out during lesson time, meaning that pupils are withdrawn from classroom learning? Which lessons will they be withdrawn from?*
- *How will we ensure that teachers are aware of the tasks and learning objectives of the intervention sessions?*
- *How will teachers make best use of and extend the learning gained from intervention sessions? How can they integrate it into whole-class contexts (e.g. teacher input and group work)?*

Primary school leaders should also consider whether the interventions are timely. Early intervention often has the most profound effect; so wherever possible, aim to identify learning needs and address them through the appropriate strategies before pupils leave Key Stage 1.

If you want to improve the effectiveness of your TAs, you will need to address the questions above and include the resulting decisions in your school policy of TA deployment. Jean Gross' book, *Beating bureaucracy in special educational needs*, contains a useful toolkit for evaluating the quality of interventions.

Once choices have been made, teachers can be given the responsibility of running the intervention programmes according to the new model, maximising the effectiveness of the TAs to the benefit of the pupils they teach. You might like to consider adopting a layer approach to the delivery of some or all of your interventions. This approach involves an intervention being delivered by a teacher and a TA, with the teacher working with the lowest-attaining pupils, and the TA working with the pupils in the tier above – those who are struggling, but not as needy as the lowest attainers. Some interventions are designed with this approach in mind, and require both teacher and TA to have specialist training; however, you may be able to remodel existing interventions in a similar way.

Key recommendations on interventions

- Carry out a systematic evaluation of all the interventions delivered by TAs. Based on this evaluation, be willing to change the location, frequency, content and duration of interventions. Abandon any interventions that are not producing benefits for pupils.
- Ensure that teachers set targets for individual pupils in relation to interventions that align with their National Curriculum targets.
- Ensure that teachers take steps to integrate the content and outcomes of interventions with class work, through increased involvement in the selection, preparation, delivery and assessment of intervention programmes.
- Ensure that TAs are encouraged to provide meaningful and systematic feedback to teachers on pupils' engagement and progress.

TAs leading classes

Some of the schools we visited as part of the DISS project (and many more who provided responses to our questionnaires) deployed TAs to lead classes as part of arrangements to release teachers for PPA and/or to cover short-term teacher absence. In secondary schools, cover supervisors often undertake lesson cover for unplanned teacher absence. Much of what we have to say in this section (and indeed throughout much of the book) can be applied to support staff working in this role (like TAs, the role of cover supervisor does not require a professional qualification, such as QTS).

One of the most contentious issues arising out of the National Agreement was TAs leading classes. In a very visible way, TAs were seen to replace teachers, even though the nature of the work – labelled 'supervision' – was described in such a way as to make it distinct from 'teaching'. However, from our research on the DISS project, it was clear that when TAs led classes, they took on a teaching role – much as they did when they were working with individuals or groups. In many cases, this was inevitable, as pupils, keen to get on with the work left for them by the teacher – asked TAs questions related to tasks and required explanations of concepts.

Leading classes gives the TA a role that obviously overlaps with that of the teacher, in terms of having class-level responsibility and interactions. The aim of the restructuring process described in this book is to create roles for TAs that are distinct from the teachers' role, and so you must be absolutely clear about your expectations of what TAs can and cannot do and what you want them to achieve when deployed to lead classes, and this must be shared with your staff.

If you decide to deploy TAs in roles that put them in charge of classes, without the presence of a teacher, you must be very deliberate in your choice of the individual(s) to whom you assign this role. You may even wish to assign a pair of TAs to lead a class, so they can support one another. Although, as we shall explain, a process of training for TAs may be necessary for some TAs who do not, at present, have the full skills set to thrive in the role in which you wish to place them, the supervision role is something of a special case. It is likely that leading classes will not be something that every TA in your school will wish to do; it takes a particular level of confidence to command a class of 30 pupils, especially if the culture of behaviour and/or respect for adults in the school is not all that it could be. TAs we have spoken to as part of the DISS and EDTA projects, describe the damage to their confidence sustained by comments from pupils that undermine TAs: typically, 'You're not a proper teacher'.

Primary school leaders could consider developing a specific TA role(s) along the lines of a cover supervisor to take on lesson cover and/or PPA cover more or less full time. You should identify the TA(s) in your school who are willing to take on this role – and make them able. Accreditation against the HLTA standards can be used as a benchmark for determining an individual's competence in leading whole classes.

The evidence from the DISS project is quite clear: the effectiveness of TAs and cover supervisors hinges on the quality of preparation provided; not just in terms of training in classroom management, but also in terms of wider systems for sharing lesson information. We will return to this in Chapter 4.

Key recommendations on TAs leading classes

- Ask yourself: Is the climate conducive to this kind of role in my school? Will the pupils accept TAs leading classes?
- Be absolutely clear about the limitations of TAs deployed to lead classes. They are *not* teachers, so calibrate your expectations accordingly. Ensure teachers are clear on this too.
- Consider creating a designated 'cover TA' role for your strongest TA(s).

Class-, year- or subject-based TAs

The allocation of TAs to particular classes, year groups or subject departments is necessarily a school-level decision made by you and your SLT. Having established, via the audit, the present model of allocation, your review will need to consider its underpinning aims and objectives. Evaluations of current effectiveness and changes to particular aims or objectives should lead to alterations in the deployment of some or all of your TAs. It might be that models can coexist. For example, if you are in a primary school, it may be more appropriate to have class-based TAs in Key Stage 1 and year-based TAs in Key Stage 2. If you run a large secondary school, you may even consider having your most knowledgeable subject-based TAs attached to Key Stage 4 to support pupils in the build-up to exams.

As we have noted, we strongly recommend that, as a school, you move away from the individual-based TA model (e.g. the Velcro model). Here, therefore, we look in turn at deployment for TAs who are predominantly based in classes, year groups and subject departments.

CLASS-BASED TAs

A school system where TAs are class based presents some advantages. Continuity, for example, means that there is greater opportunity for the teacher-TA partnership to develop. It also allows adults to become more familiar with the pupils' attitudes to learning and behaviour, and their particular learning needs.

However, the DISS project findings revealed some potential disadvantages for teachers and pupils from this model of deployment. First, we found that teachers could avoid taking direct responsibility for some aspects of their teaching, in terms of leaving tasks to be prepared and taught by TAs, especially interventions, for example. Second, we discovered that there is a risk that teachers assume that the TA is so familiar with the way they work that explanations or explicit expectations are not required. This failure to make the tacit knowledge that teachers possess explicit to TAs impedes TAs' capacity to work in ways that advance pupil learning.

You will need to alert teachers who work with class-based TAs about the potential dangers of separation from teachers, and support them to develop alternative ways of deploying TAs (see section on classroom-level decisions that follows). Leaving individual teachers to make choices in isolation is not adequate, and such practice has unquestionably led to the situation described in the DISS project, where there is a distinct lack of coordination and consistency in TA use across the school; in secondary schools this issue is particularly acute. Your school policy should be clear on how class-based TAs are to be deployed.

YEAR GROUP-BASED TAs

It may be that you choose to allocate TAs to year groups or Key Stages, rather than classes. This can reduce the dangers inherent in the latter form of deployment, as we have described. Some year groups may merit a greater number of TAs, or more TA time. These considerations will be part of your deployment choice process and you should clearly explain and justify your rationale for these decisions to the teachers working in each year group.

TAs have the advantage of becoming familiar with the curriculum content, schemes of work, expected range of pupil outcomes and forms of assessment designed for the specific year group to which they are attached. There may be other aspects, such as models of classroom organisation and expected levels of pupil independence, with which TAs can become conversant, and which will be consistent across all the classes in the year. In secondary schools, the spread of pupil attainment is likely to widen over Key Stages 3 and 4 (and with it, the demands of their tasks), so allocation to a single year group might be more appropriate.

It is worth noting that some of the risks associated with the class-based TA model as described are also relevant to this context, and so you must be mindful of them if you use the year-based model. Also, if you deploy TA across several classes, you will need to reflect this in the amount of pre-lesson preparation time you allocate.

SUBJECT-BASED TAs

Secondary schools typically operate a departmental structure, organising teaching and assessment into curriculum subjects – both singly (e.g. maths) and in groups (e.g. expressive arts). It may be your choice to allocate TAs to departments and leave the detailed decisions regarding how individual TAs are deployed within each subject to your heads of department, through consultation with their staff. However, the school policy on TA deployment must explicitly set the parameters for such mid-level decision-making, setting out the criteria for such decisions, along with clear expectations for how the TAs can be used by teachers to aid pupil progress. It must also be clear on how TAs are *not* to be used.

The advantages for secondary schools of deploying TAs in this way are fairly self-evident: there is a narrower range of subject content with which to be conversant; the same is true of the syllabus, set texts, assessment criteria and exam formats; and there are fewer pupils to teach each week, so familiarity with them and their needs is that much easier. TAs in schools that we know have moved to this model are also much more likely to be included in the life of the department, and are welcomed to department meetings. This has obvious benefits for TAs in terms of feeling valued.

Teachers can also become more used to planning for, and working in collaboration with, individual TAs who will regularly be deployed in their classrooms. Growing knowledge of, and trust in, the qualities and abilities of departmental TAs can be a benefit to teachers and pupils alike.

However, in developing this school-level model of TA deployment, you will need to consider issues of the suitability of individuals (in terms of their level of subject knowledge) and preparedness for a teaching role (in terms of their pedagogical knowledge). It should not be assumed that having a degree in a particular subject means that TAs will be effective teachers of it. For TAs located in English and maths departments, training to deliver specific interventions may be necessary.

Case study

Subject-based TAs

One secondary school in the EDTA project restructured its use of TAs, moving from a model of deployment where TAs operated from a physically separated Learning Support provision and supporting pupils with SEN across the curriculum, to a model where TAs were based in subject departments in the main school building. The TAs who participated in the project were two of only a small number of TAs who had been subject-based for at least one year already, and were able to be advocates for the benefits of being located within a faculty (e.g. in terms of greater opportunities for communicating with teachers and building deeper subject knowledge).

Key recommendations class-, year- or subject-based TAs

- The model of the Velcro TA is no longer an option. Explore the options of deploying TAs in predominantly class-based, year group-based or subject department-based roles.
- Be mindful of the risks associated with class- and year-based models in particular (e.g. pupils' dependency on TAs and separation from the teacher).
- Ensure that the deployment decisions that will be devolved to teachers and/or heads of department are clearly framed within your school policy on TA deployment, and set the expectations and limits of what is acceptable. This will greatly enhance the coordination and consistency of TA use across the school.
- Be aware that deploying TAs across a greater number of classes/teachers will have implications for the amount of time needed for pre- and post-lesson communication.

TAs' conditions of employment and TA recruitment

The DISS project found that decisions about TAs' contracts and hours of work had a strong bearing on how TAs were deployed and prepared, and this is captured in the WPR model. So, once the school has reviewed its deployment decisions, based on the most relevant and important criteria, it may be that the issues of recruitment and conditions of employment are also found to be in need of attention.

The job description associated with each TA role – those that are predominantly pedagogical, nurturing roles, care roles (e.g. supporting pupils with mobility difficulties) and so on – will demand different sets of recruitment and selection criteria.

Auditing your present TA workforce will reveal strengths and also gaps, which should feed directly into your recruitment process. In particular, decisions about what TAs in pedagogical roles are employed to achieve will need to be made prior to setting out job descriptions and adding new recruits to the TA workforce.

The specific nature of any vacant TA roles you are seeking to fill must be made explicit in adverts and recruitment materials. The selection criteria must be clear in terms of what qualifications and skills, as well as experience (if applicable), the appointment will be based on. For pedagogical roles, the interview process must also reflect the emphasis on teaching. Many candidates who in the past may have been appointed, or thought suitable to be TAs, will be seen in a new light with these tighter, more demanding criteria being applied. A new breed of TAs may be what your school needs, and we are aware of a number of schools, particularly secondary schools, which are benefiting from employing graduates with subject-specific skills and knowledge. Furthermore, working as a TA can be a desirable part-time role for students taking undergraduate or postgraduate courses.

We are also aware of schools that are tapping into local expertise in the form of qualified teachers who are returning to work after taking time out to raise the children. Parents with young children may not wish to take on a part-time but nonetheless demanding teaching role, and therefore a part-time TA role may suit their childcare needs, while adding capacity to your pupil support workforce. TAs with QTS might be willing to take on the delivery of curriculum interventions or lead booster groups.

We have termed this new approach to TA recruitment as 'year zero', meaning that schools are resetting the clock and will henceforth select TAs according to more rigorous standards.

Case study

Raising the bar

One primary school that participated in the EDTA project has seen the quality of applicants for TA vacancies greatly improve, due to the way in which posts are advertised. There is a stronger set of expectations set out from the start; job descriptions are much clearer; the interview process is more rigorous; as is the induction process, with training provided by the HLTAs. There is a formal system of performance management in place for TAs, which includes an audit. TAs who do well are being used to provide peer support through observation. The school has become a local beacon of good practice, visited by TAs from other schools. The experience has been good for TAs' morale.

By choosing to give TAs a pedagogical role, you are obligated to be concerned about their competence as teachers. New recruits are an ideal way to face this reality and raise the bar by setting minimum entry levels to the role. As a result of participation in the EDTA project, a number of the schools we worked with set minimum expectations for qualifications for new appointees. One primary school, for example, changed its recruitment policy so that it would only consider graduates for vacant TA posts.[8] For TA posts that are principally pedagogical roles, setting the bar for entry in this way puts greater emphasis on the teaching that the school expects TAs to carry out. It makes explicit what has previously been implicit; teaching pupils requires drawing on one's knowledge, understanding and skills. Previously, this reality was neglected. As many headteachers told us in the DISS project, they tended to make appointments based on impressions and assumptions that successful candidates 'had what it takes'; rarely did they describe anything more rigorous. If we are serious about raising the esteem of the TA workforce, this second-rate approach to recruitment must end.

The TAs who are currently in post present you with some particular challenges. A review and possible changes to job descriptions must be carried out in order for the school to address the TAs' levels of preparedness, particularly those with a pedagogical role. If you are unable to align some individuals with certain roles, changes in deployment will be necessary.

The process of reform, in some schools at least, is very likely to include dispensing with certain roles that exist at present. You may find yourself in a position where some of the TAs in your school do not, at present, have the competencies to fill the roles you want to establish. Or some TAs may not wish to fulfil the role you have in mind. This will be a matter for the individual. We do not underestimate the fact that there may be difficult choices involved in undertaking the systemic programme of restructuring we are advocating in this book, but, as educationalists, we have to put the needs of pupils first. If redundancies are likely, we recommend that you seek advice on employment law.

However, we stress that it is the *roles* that are to be done away with and not the individuals who occupy them. In fairness to TAs, the role has historically grown around them and, as the DISS project has shown, has not been accompanied with the necessary support to help them adjust. This is why we would advocate a process of training to support TAs to grow into the new roles you create.

In support of this more professionalised approach to managing and organising TAs, there is one further consideration worth mentioning here. We will deal with changes to improve TA preparation in Chapter 4, but taking preparedness seriously will often necessitate changes to working hours. You may need to extend the TAs' working day at the start, the end or both, and this may be problematic for some individuals. Again, these are matters that it will be up to the individual to deal with. TAs who accept this new arrangement are likely to require new or updated contracts of employment, starting from the next school year. For new recruits, the hours of work you wish to introduce can be made clear during the application process so that they are able to make an informed choice about whether they would be willing to accept the conditions of employment associated with the role.

The school policy on TAs should express clearly what the TA roles are, what the selection criteria must be, and include examples of the job descriptions for the roles you create. Teachers and TAs should all be fully aware of the policy, so that deployment decisions, preparation and performance review processes, are all integrated in order to maximise the effectiveness of TAs' contributions to pupils' learning.

Key recommendations on TAs' conditions of employment and TA recruitment

- Adopt a 'year zero' approach to TA recruitment. Approach the future recruitment of TAs differently, raising the entry level qualifications and making clear the expected hours of work.
- These arrangements should be formally expressed in a job description and person specification. The new standards and expectations should be defined by, and set out in, the school's policy for TA deployment.
- Conditions of employment will need to be reviewed for existing TAs and for all future contracts, in support of changes in TA roles, particularly those relating to changes to working hours.
- Make every effort to train TAs who are currently in post if they do not possess the full skills set required for the role in which you wish to deploy them.

The choices and decisions you and your SLT make to affect school-level change should be seen as an outcome of the desire to make TAs more effective in enhancing pupils' progress.

Choices about TA deployment: classroom-level decisions

The guidance contained in this section is aimed at teachers. You may be a school leader or teacher working in a school considering or undertaking a reform of TA deployment, in which case this section will add more detail in terms of how school-wide changes might translate to the classroom. In this book, we are encouraging school leaders to develop a policy on TA deployment, based on a thorough audit of current practice, which will set in place a structure within which teachers can make more informed choices about how to deploy TAs in their classrooms. However, you may be reading this book as a teacher or trainee teacher working in a school that (as far as you know) is not considering such a process of restructuring (in which case, you might want anonymously to leave a copy of this book in your headteacher's pigeonhole!), and are looking for advice on how to improve your own practice with regard to TAs. Here, then, we focus on the decisions facing teachers who wish to affect change at the classroom level.

Adding value

There are two fundamental points that teachers must have in mind when considering how to deploy TAs in the classroom. If the school has set in place a policy of TA deployment, in line with our recommendations, the fundamental question about whether the TA role is overtly pedagogical or non-pedagogical in nature will have been answered, and this will frame your choices at the class level. If there is no such structure in place, you should impose your own limits on what you expect TAs to do in your classroom, and in ways they will 'add value' to what you do. In this section (and in the sections on class-level decisions in the following two chapters), we will set aside the notion of an overarching school-level policy and concentrate on the aspects of deployment that are within teachers' power to change.

Our way of conceptualising this is to envisage the classroom as it would be with you (the teacher), but without the TA. How will you organise things in order to provide the best educational experience for *all* pupils in the class (e.g. via quality first teaching), including those typically supported by the TA? Following this, think about your additional resource – your TA – being reintroduced to the classroom. What can he/she do that helps you to help teaching and learning, and/or to help keep the classroom running efficiently and effectively – *without* replacing you?

Key recommendations on adding value

- Consider ways in which the TA can 'add value' to your role, where they do not, in effect, replace 'the teacher'.
- Ensure you retain the responsibility for the learning of *all* pupils, and TAs are deployed to help keep the classroom running efficiently and effectively.

Defining the non-pedagogical roles for TAs

Supporting teachers

The DISS project showed that teachers readily acknowledge the help provided by TAs (and other support staff) in completing many non-pedagogical tasks, in terms of their contribution to improving teachers' job satisfaction and decreasing their workload and feelings of stress.

When TAs take on teachers' routine clerical tasks (e.g. photocopying, filing, etc.), it frees up time for teachers to focus on teaching tasks, such as lesson planning or assessment. This, in turn, improves their teaching. We refer to this form of TA support as having an *indirect* impact on pupils; TAs help teachers to help pupils.

If you wish to deploy TAs to take on your routine tasks, you will need to define which tasks you want them to perform; there may be some that you wish to retain, such as classroom display (we found this to be the case in the DISS project). The tasks may, to some extent, have a degree of regularity and pattern to them, but they will also inevitably have an element of variety, reflecting the work of the pupils and the teacher across the school year.

One further consideration might be to think about which of these routine tasks pupils could do. If building their independence and self-efficacy is a key aim for you, you might like to have a set of jobs for which pupils can be responsible; for example, preparing and tidying away art materials, and tidying areas of the classroom.

Another expression of this *indirect* form of pupil support provided by TAs – and appreciated by teachers – is in terms of classroom management. Low-level disruption that disrupts the flow of your lessons and becomes wearing can be greatly reduced when TAs are deployed to manage this kind of off-task behaviour and ensure that pupils are focused, attentive and on-task. This gives you more time to teach, thus benefiting pupils.

The teacher must remain in control of motivating pupils, gaining and maintaining their focus, and be responsible for behaviour management overall (and especially for serious incidents). However, there are ways in which the TA can watch for those small signs of negative and off-task behaviour, and step in to address it without disrupting your delivery or the flow of the lesson.

This form of TA deployment will need to be both sensitive and responsive to the emerging needs of the pupils across any particular lesson. TAs are used to sitting as part of the class audience and can pick up on things that teachers do not always notice, because teachers are focused on teaching.

This form of support may be unnecessary if low-level disruption is not an issue in your class, or if you prefer to deal with it yourself. Therefore, the nature and limits of this behaviour monitoring role need to be made explicit to each TA in each teaching and learning context; Year 9 last lesson on a Friday may be notorious for low-level disruption, whereas Year 7 on Monday morning may be quite the reverse.

You will have to agree with your TA the appropriate forms of intervention. In the most effective instances we have seen, TAs are able to discreetly capture the attention of disruptive or off-task pupils, and with a look, a gesture or a whisper, quell the disquiet. We have seen many examples of TAs dampen potentially volatile situations, refocus off-task pupils, break up chatter, confiscate sweets, move pupils to other seats, and even send them from the room, limit the distracting effects of individual pupils, and generally keep the classroom ticking over, allowing the teacher to teach and pupils to learn. You must decide the limits of what TAs will be allowed to do; for example, you may be happy for them to move a pupil to another desk, but not to send them from the classroom.

You may wish to include the TA in your sanctions and rewards policy, allowing them to award points for behaviour. But ensure there is consistency; pupils are quick to pick up on variations in punishments for the same misdemeanour.

While you have the ultimate responsibility for the management of behaviour in the classroom, your pupils will need to know that the TA is acting as your enforcer. It will need to be clear to them that you have given the TA the power to deal with low-level disruption and that he/she is to be respected and obeyed in this capacity. You must demonstrate that you are a team and that you back his/her judgement. In the worst cases we have seen and had described to us, pupils undermine both the teacher, and particularly the TA, when they divide and rule, playing the teacher's seniority off against the TA's relatively weaker position.

Presenting yourself as a united force will help, along with a consistent approach to reprimand and rewards, but so will training and support from you. This is what really gives TAs confidence. You will need to coach and mentor them in classroom management techniques, and again, to achieve the best effects, it should be in line with whole-school strategies for managing behaviour.

Supporting pupils' physical and emotional needs

In many ways, the role of TAs assigned to support pupils' physical and emotional needs are decisions made at the school level and involve activity that takes place away from the classroom, such as helping pupils to move around the school building, physiotherapy or interventions led by Emotional Literacy Support Assistants. Such support can be considered to have an *indirect* impact on pupil learning, as it helps pupils to access teaching and learning in a physical and/or dispositional sense.

As noted, some forms of support for physical needs are less likely to take place in classrooms. Nonetheless, there will be some activities that do; for example, TAs who sign for pupils with hearing impairments, or assist pupils with visual impairments.

While we do not understate the need for necessary forms of physical support, our research has raised concerns about the assumptions teachers of mainstream classes make about the need for and level of support they should provide for pupils with physical needs. Although it is true that many pupils with physical needs do not have learning needs, many do. And although TAs who support such pupils have often had specialist training to assist pupils' physical needs, it should not be assumed that they have had quality training to support their learning needs as well (Anderson and Finney 2008; Lamb 2009; and Norwich and Lewis 2001). Michael Giangreco (2003) refers to this as the 'training trap': the tendency for teachers to relinquish instruction of pupils with SEN to TAs who have received more or less any kind of training, no matter how scant. We would also add that some school leaders and teachers also fall into the trap when they assume that holding an advanced qualification (e.g. an A level or degree) in a particular subject indicates anything at all about a TA's ability to teach and to advance learning.

This clearly speaks to issues concerning the preparedness of TAs, which we shall address in Chapter 4. However, the two points to make here are that when teachers fall into the training trap, it increases the separation between teachers and TA-supported pupils, and pupils can develop an unhelpful dependency on the TA. This dependency damages the development of pupils' independent skills.

So, are there other things that TAs could be doing when they are in the classroom with you, and are not needed to provide physical support to pupils? The audit tools in Chapter 2 will help you to determine the extent to which TAs spend time *actually* supporting pupils' physical needs in lessons, and suggest whether the capacity exists for TAs to perform other pedagogical or non-pedagogical roles. These roles, of course, will be clearly defined by you, and supported with training and guidance from you.

In terms of supporting pupils' emotional needs, we have described how TAs have the sensitivity, instincts and mannerisms well suited to supporting pupils' pastoral needs, and it may be that you can profit from this in the classroom by modifying the way TAs interact with pupils. We will return to this in Chapter 5.

Key recommendations on defining the non-pedagogical roles of TAs

- When thinking about how TAs can add value to your teaching, capitalise on things TAs are better placed to do (e.g. monitor behaviour).
- Look for efficiencies in TA time. Are there other things they could be doing when they are not, for example, supporting pupils' physical needs?
- Clearly define the remit of non-pedagogical roles; for example, in terms of the tasks that you would like TAs to do and not to do; for example, the appropriate level of intervention in managing behaviour.
- Ensure pupils are clear about the role of the TA and that you support him/her.
- Ensure that any role change or extension is supported by training and is consistent with school policy (e.g. on behaviour management).

Defining the pedagogical role of TAs

In line with the general picture revealed through our research, it is likely that you currently deploy TAs in your classroom in a pedagogical role, and you may wish to continue to do so; however, the message so far in this book is clear: if you are deploying TAs in the ways described in Chapter 1, this has to change in order for your pupils to benefit from instructional interactions with TAs.

The evidence from the EDTA project shows that such change has significant benefits for teachers too. This section follows a similar structure to the section on school-level decisions about the pedagogical role of the TA, and considers the implications for some of the issues raised in that section for class teachers. We shall express these issues as questions for you to consider, before exploring each in turn.

1 *What role should the TA have in supporting lower-attaining pupils and, in particular, those with SEN?*

2 *What is the role of TAs – and teachers – in planning, delivering and assessing intervention programmes?*

3 *How can you make best use of TAs deployed to classes, year groups and/or subjects?*

You may decide that some TAs you work with should have greater pedagogical responsibilities than others, if, for example, they have particular strengths in specific subject areas. But, as we suggested, do not assume that holding a GCSE or A level qualification, for instance, means that a TA is able to teach or advance learning in a certain subject.

You must determine the limitations of the pedagogical role. There may be some circumstances under which the TA's teaching role has near parity with your own teaching role, but you must be mindful not to delegate your responsibility for advancing the learning of *all* pupils.

As we noted, our research has revealed that many teachers have a view about the encroachment of TAs on their professional teaching role – some are more positive than others (see Blatchford, Russell and Webster 2012) – but rarely do they look this issue full in the face and make decisions about how it affects their classroom practice. This section will guide you through that process.

TAs and pupils with SEN

The DISS project findings showed that TAs had a primary role in teaching lower-attaining pupils and those with SEN. Rather than providing teaching and support that is additional to that from teachers, teaching and support from TAs is an *alternative* to that from teachers. To qualify as additional support, TA-supported pupils would have to have at least as much input from teachers as their peers, but the DISS project data shows that this is not the case: TAs are to a large extent deployed *in place of* teachers.

In both the DISS and EDTA projects, we found a worrying tendency for teachers – particularly those in secondary schools – to assume that meeting the learning and behavioural needs of pupils with SEN is the responsibility of someone else, often the Learning Support department. This is especially the case among teachers of subjects other than English and maths – subjects for which there is a high amount of literacy and numeracy intervention input from TAs for lower-attaining pupils and those with SEN.

It bears repeating that it is you – the teacher – who is responsible for the progress and development of pupils in your charge. The Learning Support department can help you to achieve better outcomes for pupils, but it is not for the people who work in there (who are mostly TAs, let us not forget) to do your job for you.

Your deployment of TAs has implications for your own classroom practice. As we stated, the challenge to you, as a class teacher, is to consider ways in which TAs can add value to your classroom duties and responsibilities. In other words, think first of all about what you should be doing to support lower-attaining pupils and those with SEN, and then use the TA in ways that help you to facilitate that.

A major issue revealed by the DISS project was the separation of TA-supported pupils from the teacher and the curriculum. You must consider how to organise your own teaching and that of the TA, in order to avoid this.

In the first instance, you need to question the notion of asking or allowing TAs to withdraw pupils from the class to work on tasks that are the same as or differentiated from what the rest of the class is doing. This was a common arrangement we have witnessed in a number of classrooms, and it must be avoided wherever possible.

In most cases, however, the changes you will need to consider concern the allocation of individual pupils or groups to work with the TA in a remedial role. Changes you make will need to reverse the situation commonly found in the DISS project: you must become the adult with whom pupils with SEN have regular, sustained and focused interactions. Rather than routinely assigning the TA to teach the pupils whose learning needs are greatest and most demanding – and therefore require professional input – you will have to ensure that the TA works with pupils across the class as a whole, thereby allowing you the opportunity to interact regularly with these pupils, and for sustained periods. Teachers in the EDTA project greatly improved and enriched their understanding of the learning needs and progress of lower-attaining pupils and those with SEN, who previously worked more often with the TA than the teacher.

This type of shift in TA deployment is fundamental, but as the teachers in the EDTA project found, not just beneficial, but relatively simple to implement. Their strategies reduced pupils' separation from them, from the curriculum, and from peers.

You too can address the tendency for TAs to have a remedial role, routinely supporting lower-attaining groups and pupils with SEN, by widening the range of contexts in which they are deployed. Instead, use TAs to support groups of gifted and talented pupils, average-attaining pupils, and mixed ability groups.

You may even consider deploying yourself and your TA on a rotational basis, so that both adults work with a different group each day throughout the week. Of course, if you have lessons where there is more than one TA present, you widen your options. One successful version of this model we observed in the EDTA project had the teacher setting independent and group work tasks for the tables without an adult present. Over the course of the week, each table had the same amount of time being supported by the teacher, supported by the TA, working in a group and working independently.

As a teacher, you probably move about the classroom when the pupils are working, ensuring that pupils are on-task and progressing; this is what we call 'roving'. As you are doing this, the TA may be working with a lower-attaining group or individual. Have you thought about reversing roles? Or you may like to consider developing a roving role for the TA as well – that way, you can cover more pupils. The swapping or alternating of roles had broad support from teachers and TAs who participated in the EDTA project. One model we observed allowed the TA to bring to the attention of the teacher particular individuals whom she saw were having difficulty with the task. Once alerted, the teacher moved in to provide targeted support while the TA continued to rove.

Depending on the particular skills of the TAs you work with and their suitability to these roles, these ideas – all drawn from work undertaken in real classrooms – can be used in different combinations, depending on the lesson, the tasks and needs of the pupils in each class you teach.

It is worth noting that these strategies support what Ofsted inspectors look for in the best lessons: 'Resources ... make a marked contribution to the quality of learning, as does the precisely targeted support provided by other adults' (2011a). Furthermore, inspectors with the responsibility for assessing SEN will be looking for:

- Whether TAs always work with the lowest-attaining group,
- Which stages of learning the teacher becomes involved in with pupils with SEN who are frequently supported by TAs,
- What interaction the teacher has with pupils with SEN,
- Whether TA-supported pupils are prevented from interacting with other pupils.

Working with pupils in a pedagogical role across the attainment range, in a one-to-one, group or roving capacity, all present particular challenges. Therefore, such changes to the ways TAs are deployed will need to be accompanied by training. If your school is making wholesale changes to TA deployment, this may be addressed more formally at that school level, but if not, you will need to provide the necessary guidance, at the outset and on an ongoing basis.

Indeed, in moving to models of classroom organisation, which will give you more opportunities to work with pupils with SEN, you may require some specific training to raise your own knowledge and understanding of the needs of these pupils (e.g. particular types of SEN), and developing your pedagogical skills in this area.

At the core of the strategies you use and develop with regard to TAs' classroom deployment must remain the notion that whatever pedagogical role you assign to TAs, it should be monitored by you to ensure that there is a fairer balance of teacher-pupil time across the attainment range, and that TAs are not being asked to work outside their current level of competency.

Key recommendations on defining the pedagogical role of TAs

- Watch for the signs of ineffective deployment, such as evidence of pupil dependency on TAs.
- Consider the ways in which you deploy *yourself* in lessons, in terms of the groups you tend to support.
- Ensure that lower-attaining pupils and those with SEN are not routinely and unnecessarily separated from you and the classroom.
- Ensure that lower-attaining pupils and those with SEN receive at least as much time with you as other pupils. Consider rotating the groups you and the TA work with across the week.
- Consider additional classroom organisation strategies that do not require adult support, for example peer-led group work.

TAs and intervention programmes

The DISS project called attention to the way TA-led, out-of-class interventions separate pupils from the teacher and classroom. Furthermore, the widespread lack of teacher involvement with, and general ignorance of, the content, teaching and outcomes of many interventions meant that they are unable to integrate or build on them in their class teaching. TAs, we found, were not adept at doing this either, so it was left to pupils to make connections between their learning in interventions and their learning in the classroom.

Research on the use of TAs to deliver intervention projects (e.g. by Alborz *et al.* 2009) is clear on the positive impact on pupil attainment, as long as they are properly prepared and supported. But, in its current form, the use of TAs in such a way that they often select, plan, deliver and assess interventions is failing to have the wider impact we would want to see, in terms of progress in literacy, for example, over a school year. It is these signs of wider integration into the curriculum that Ofsted inspectors look for (Ofsted 2011b).

In some schools, teachers have less control over the deployment of TAs to lead interventions; as we have stated; in secondary schools, this is often handled by the Learning Support department, and overseen by the SENCO. However effective these centrally run processes are, you should not become detached from them. Therefore, if you deploy your TA to carry out interventions, or there is a wider school policy of doing so, you will need to review your involvement in this arrangement and become more informed about:

- The broad aims and effectiveness of intervention programmes
- The specific objectives of individual intervention sessions
- The extent to which pupils achieve these aims and objectives, and to what extent these aims match their National Curriculum targets set by you.

You will also, as far as you are able, need to become involved in:

- The selection, preparation and assessment of the intervention sessions
- Decisions about where and when TAs deliver the programmes. If pupils need to be withdrawn from lessons, which lessons will they be withdrawn from?
- Improving the teaching approaches used by TAs
- Possible involvement in the delivery of interventions; for example, via the layered approach (as explained in the section on school-level decisions)
- Establishing a process of specific and regular (if possible, daily) feedback from TAs on pupil performance
- Integrating and extending the learning gained from intervention sessions in your classroom interactions (e.g. your teaching input and work with individuals and groups).

Some teachers in the EDTA project trialled targeted one-to-one tutorials for pupils with SEN, with a view to improving the interventions carried out by TAs. Some schools carried out a 'health check', evaluating the effectiveness of interventions delivered by TAs, and dropped those that had little or no impact. As a consequence, these schools were in a position to reduce the number of out-of-class interventions taking place and a shift towards a greater use of TAs in classrooms.

In line with our suggestions regarding TAs and pupils with SEN, you might be able to explore the prospect of delivering some interventions yourself, in the classroom, while the TA roves or supervises the class.

We found that in classes where teachers and TAs had trained in the same interventions, there was a greater integration of the learning achieved by pupils in the intervention sessions with their classroom experience. Being fully aware of the content and the outcomes enables teachers to make use of facts, concepts, skills and understanding in their teaching. This will increase the chances of the pupils' learning being consolidated, applied and extended, and maximising the potential long-term benefits of the interventions taught by TAs.

Key recommendations on interventions

- Be informed about the interventions that are used in your school.
- Plan and prepare intervention sessions with TAs, and be mindful of when and where they take place.
- Ensure that the targets you set for individual pupils relating to interventions align with their National Curriculum targets.
- Get regular feedback from TAs on pupil performance in interventions and use this to inform your lesson planning and classroom interactions.

Class-, year- or subject-based TAs

We have already touched on some of the models of class-level deployment in the section on TAs and pupils with SEN (e.g. in terms of TAs roving the room and working with different attainment groups). So here, we will look at the other ways in which you can make the most of TAs who are predominantly based in classes, year groups and subject departments.

CLASS-BASED TAs

Class-based TAs present some advantages. Continuity, for example, allows you to develop a partnership with your TA, and TAs can become more familiar with the pupils in the class, in terms of their attitudes to learning and behaviour, and their particular learning needs. But the advantages to you are only as good as the models of TA deployment you use.

The work conducted for the EDTA project showed that teachers can derive significant benefits from making simple changes to the way they deploy TAs.

First, simply having an awareness of the effects of ineffective forms of TA deployment meant that teachers were much more mindful of reducing the use of these models in their classroom practice. Teachers who often sent or allowed TAs to work with individuals and groups outside the class did this far less.

Awareness of findings from the pre-intervention observations meant that a number of teachers used the three-part lesson structure to help devise specific roles for TAs at different stages of the lesson. (You will recall that identifying the lesson part is a feature of the observation schedule shown in Chapter 2.)

The three-part structure – teacher input, main learning task and plenary – presents opportunities for you to deploy TAs in different ways. We have already covered the different roles TAs could perform during the main learning task in the section on TAs and pupils with SEN, so let us look at what we learned from the EDTA project participants in relation to TA deployment during teacher input.

Before changes were made as part of the EDTA project, our pre-intervention data revealed that when TAs were in the classroom, teachers spent more than half of their time talking to the whole class. During these times, TAs were what we call 'passive': listening to the teacher teach, and having brief intermittent interactions with pupils. As one secondary school TA told us:

> *If you're just kind of not doing anything, and the teacher's stood there reading from a book and things like that, and then they'll start asking the class questions ... you can't really do an awful lot, can you? If that goes on for near enough the whole lesson, what can you do?*

Again, once this was brought to teachers' attention, they did things differently in a bid to make better use of TAs' time during their input.

Some teachers deployed the TA in a more prominent role during their input, ensuring that the TA had been prepared in advance. In one primary classroom, the TA took notes on the whiteboard, allowing the teacher to remain facing the class and more able to identify pupils who showed signs of not understanding the concept or task, and to respond to any off-task, inattentive behaviour that she would have missed with her back turned.

Case study

An enhanced role for TA

The TA in one secondary classroom had been given a more prominent role at the front of the class, and did tasks for the teacher, such as writing notes on the whiteboard and asking pre-prepared questions in turn with the teacher. This form of deployment had two notable effects. First, the notes on the board were made primarily for the benefit of a pupil in the class with dyslexia, which avoided the often stigmatising effect of the TA sitting beside the pupil taking notes for him; plus it began to reverse the tendency for him to depend on the TA, and gave him the opportunity and independence to practise his handwriting. Second, the small, well-defined role the TA had in lesson delivery allowed her to display her significant subject knowledge, thus challenging the view held by some pupils in the class that the TA was 'less knowledgeable' than the teacher.

Some teachers made a more conscious effort to model good teaching or questioning for TAs during their input. TAs made notes on key words, relevant questions and instructional techniques that they used when working with a group during the main learning task. This is in stark contrast to the common picture we found in the DISS project, where TAs are expected to 'tune in' to the teacher's classroom talk and make their own decisions about what is needed to support pupils with tasks.

Several teachers instructed TAs to watch and take notes on a particular pupil, or to observe peer-to-peer interactions. This information was later fed back to the teacher.

The lesson plenaries we observed tended to be quite short, and there was less evidence of teachers having developed a particular role for TAs during these periods. Often, TAs continued to work with an individual or group, or collected in resources. As plenaries are whole-class, teacher-led sessions, some of the suggestions relating to TA deployment during the main input may apply here (e.g. TAs using the whiteboard).

YEAR GROUP-BASED TAs

Allocation of TAs on a year group basis can aid the teachers in avoiding some of the dangers of having a class-based TA with them more or less all the time. But deployment of TAs across more than one class, which is common in secondary schools, can lead to inconsistencies that, in turn, have a bearing on the effectiveness of TAs.

Discussion between teachers in a particular year group can benefit all concerned because it opens up the chances of sharing planning, preparation of resources, coverage of the schemes of work, as well as developing the new models of TA deployment. TAs are well positioned to act as conduits to inform teachers about how different pupils behave and progress in different lessons, with different teachers. Overall, though, TAs deployed to work across classes in a particular year group or Key Stage stand to benefit teachers and pupils in ways similar to those already described for class-based TAs.

SUBJECT-BASED TAs

Teachers in secondary schools will mostly feel the advantages connected with this model of TA deployment. Teachers in subject departments that have been allocated one or more TAs will need to explore how best to deploy them and develop a consistent department-wide approach to their deployment in pedagogical roles in lessons (see guidance already given for use of class-based TAs). The knowledge, understanding and skills of individual TAs will all affect their suitability for supporting the curriculum in particular year groups.

Teachers in one secondary school that participated in the EDTA project had subject-specific TAs for science and maths. Closer working partnerships had been able to develop and were nurtured through various forms of professional development and team meetings. Subject-based TAs reported being fully included in the life of the department and being valued members of the team.

Key recommendations on class-, year- or subject-based TAs

- Be aware of the occasions when the TA(s) in your class are passive. Does this add value to your teaching?
- Consider how to use the TA in different parts of the lesson, perhaps to aid your classroom control or to pick up on specific information relevant to teaching and support. Their role can vary from lesson to lesson.
- Ensure you develop with colleagues a consistent approach to TA deployment where TAs work across two or more classes.
- Capitalise on the useful information about pupils TAs pick up when working across classes at the year group or department level.

Summary

In the last chapter of this book, we report the findings from the EDTA study on the main effects of the alternative models of TA deployment we have described here. We end this chapter by noting that over the course of the study, the schools and teachers had addressed TA deployment to such an extent that they had turned around, or were beginning to reverse, the main effects of TA deployment, as identified in the DISS project:

- Pupils who are typically supported by TAs (e.g. lower-attaining pupils and those with SEN) experienced less separation from the teacher and curriculum.
- Lower-attaining pupils and those with SEN received more input and support from teachers, either individually or as part of a group.
- At the same time, teachers were able to learn more about individual pupils' learning weaknesses and their potential.
- Teachers made better use of TA time in lessons.
- Pupils' dependency on TA support was reduced.

Chapter 4

The preparedness of TAs

Introduction

Preparedness is one of the three main components of the Wider Pedagogical Role model. As we saw in the Introduction, there are two aspects of TA preparedness:

1 TAs' overall preparation for the role of teaching;
2 TAs' day-to-day preparation for supporting particular subjects, lessons, tasks and pupils.

The findings from the DISS project concerning TA preparation, as shown in Chapter 1, are a cause for concern. It is essential, therefore, that each aspect of preparedness is reviewed and modified to ensure that TAs are better prepared for the work schools and teachers ask them to do.

In the previous chapter, we stated that decisions about deployment provide the starting point from which all other decisions about TAs flow. Having established what role you want TAs to play and how they should be deployed, you will now need to consider the appropriate forms of preparation needed for them to succeed in these roles.

In this chapter, we consider the decision-making required concerning aspects of preparation both at the school level and then at the class level. However, to avoid repetition, the guidance regarding TAs with non-pedagogical roles is covered in the school-level decisions section only.

School-level decisions on preparedness

How well prepared are your latest NQT recruits? Are they adequately prepared to teach their specialist subjects, or *all* subjects, in the case of primary school NQTs? In particular, how well has their training prepared them to meet the learning needs of their pupils with SEN, and those who underperform academically? What about the level of their day-to-day preparation? Are you aware of how well these NQTs are prepared for each day's lessons? Are you confident that their plans are clear, detailed and matched to the learning needs of their pupils? Many school leaders we meet *think* they know, but when asked *how* they know, their answers are less convincing.

Now replace the references to 'teachers' and 'NQTs' in the questions above, with 'teaching assistants', and ask the same hard questions. If you do not deploy TAs to teach your pupils – that is, they are confined to non-pedagogical roles – then these questions are not so relevant. But as we know, the DISS project showed that most TAs spend more time teaching pupils than doing anything else, so the chances are that these questions are very relevant to the situation in your school, and must be addressed as part of your wider thinking about reforming the TA role.

In Chapter 2 we set out the case for a whole-school audit on the deployment and preparation of TAs, much of which also applies to teachers. Once any inadequate or insufficient preparedness is revealed – for both TAs and teachers alike – it will be incumbent on you to address this situation as part of your rethink of the TA role. To take one example, given what the DISS project has revealed, is it reasonable, or even feasible, that a teacher with little or no knowledge of SEN can adequately deploy a TA to teach the pupils in her class who have SEN? Any attempt to shift responsibility from the teacher to the TA, in terms of being knowledgeable and skilful, must surely be resisted. Legally, the teacher is the professional responsible for the education of *every* pupil in the class.

Although improving TAs' preparedness has inevitable consequences for teachers' preparedness, in terms of how well they are able to work with and manage TAs, the purpose of this chapter is to offer guidance on how to improve the preparedness of TAs rather than teachers.

The DISS project showed that the issue of working with TAs has not been given enough attention in initial teacher training, and the preparedness of teachers is therefore as important as that of TAs. Teacher training providers must address this deficit more fully, but clearly this matter is beyond the scope of this book. Nevertheless, if you take seriously the need for teachers to plan, manage and evaluate the work of TAs successfully, you may need to provide teachers with further school-based training opportunities to help them achieve this. We highlight where this is relevant throughout this chapter.

Some important questions to ask about teachers' training

- *In your judgement, have your teachers been adequately prepared to work with and organise the TAs and other adults who work in their classrooms?*
- *Have your teachers been adequately trained to share or delegate teaching with TAs?*
- *Do you know what training your teachers have had in order to support the needs of pupils with SEN?*

As we set out in the previous chapter, the results of the audit will inform your decisions about how to deploy TAs in appropriate roles. Once this has been decided, you will need to think about how you train TAs for these roles and put in place processes and systems to support their day-to-day preparation. You will need to consider the types of preparation required for TAs in pedagogical roles and non-pedagogical roles.

Preparedness for TAs with non-pedagogical roles

Supporting teachers

Training

As we explained in the previous chapter, perhaps the most extreme expression of a non-pedagogical TA role is one in which TAs do not routinely interact with pupils. If you have chosen to create roles for TAs that help teachers with their clerical tasks, it may be necessary to offer forms of training. Some tasks, for example, data entry, will require using specific software packages. In some secondary schools, TAs may take on exam invigilation, and thus they will need to be fully conversant with the protocols of overseeing exams.

We have also explored the potential for TAs to have a behaviour management role in classrooms, which again would require some targeted training in classroom management techniques, consistent with the school's behaviour policy.

Day-to-day preparation

Daily preparation for TAs in non-pedagogical roles is unlikely to require regular meetings between teachers and TAs (although it should be mandatory if you deploy TAs in pedagogical roles). Most of what needs to be communicated can be done in a fairly ad hoc way, or through written notes. For example, we are aware of some teachers who keep a 'jobs book' in which they maintain a list of administrative tasks that TAs can do during quieter moments.

In terms of the day-to-day preparation for TAs with a behaviour monitoring role, there will be a need for teachers and TAs to share some information at the start and end of the lesson. For example, whether any pupils have had a difficult morning or experienced trouble at home the night before, and are therefore more likely to be volatile or fractious during the lesson. The teacher will mostly be aware of the behaviour incidents that will need to be followed up after a lesson, should any occur. This, therefore, reduces the need for TA feedback after the lesson. Nonetheless, TAs should be encouraged to feed back briefly before they leave the classroom any relevant information of which the teacher may not be aware.

Supporting pupils' physical and emotional needs

Training

TAs who support pupils with physical needs (e.g. mobility, visual or hearing impairment) are very likely to have already had particular training in appropriate techniques, such as handling or sign language. Following your review of TA roles, any TA deployed in such a role who has not had training will need to be trained, or to update their training if need be.

As we noted in Chapter 3, TAs are often well positioned to take on roles that support pupils' emotional needs. TAs often have the appropriate characteristics (e.g. warmth and attentiveness) required for nurturing roles. However, these cannot be considered sufficient qualifications for supporting emotional development. You will need to ensure that TAs are properly trained and qualified to take on these responsibilities. Training for programmes, such as Emotional First Aid and those delivered by ELSAs to support pupils' wellbeing, use basic counselling skills (e.g. active listening and problem clarification) to guide conversations. It is advisable that anyone undertaking high-level counselling work receives appropriate supervision from a suitably qualified person. ELSAs, for example, receive regular professional supervision from an educational psychologist.

Day-to-day preparation

There are a number of ways in which TAs supporting pupils with physical needs will need to be prepared in similar ways to TAs in pedagogical roles (which we will expand on), as they may need access to teachers' lesson resources in advance in order to make specific modifications; for example, making enlarged photocopies of worksheets for visually impaired pupils. Any prior knowledge of lesson content will help TAs to prepare in advance; for example, how they will convey particular information or concepts to hearing impaired pupils via sign language.

As with the daily preparation for TAs in behaviour monitoring roles, it will be necessary for TAs who support pupils with physical needs to share some information with teachers at the start and end of the lesson, regarding, for example, the organisation of the lesson and the classroom – will the TA need to make any particular modifications in order to ensure that the pupil can access the lesson? For pupils with emotional needs, TAs can once again inform teachers at the start of the lesson of any factors that may affect a pupil's engagement and behaviour during the lesson. In both cases, feedback from TAs at the end of the lesson will be necessary to inform future lesson planning.

It is for the headteacher and SLT to make the forms of day-to-day preparation and feedback described above obligatory throughout the school. This expectation can be written into your school policy on TA deployment. Routine feedback will enable teachers to become more informed about how pupils respond to their lessons and their teaching style, and allow them to reflect meaningfully on their practice.

Key recommendations on preparing TAs for non-pedagogical roles

- Ensure that TAs with behaviour management roles receive thorough training in classroom and pupil management techniques, which are in line with your school behaviour policy. Practice must be consistent across the school.
- TAs who have a role supporting pupils' physical and social development should receive formal training and hold the necessary qualifications to perform these roles.
- Ensure that teachers brief TAs at the start of lessons and that there are mechanisms for feedback after lessons.
- Identify a set of particular tasks (e.g. modifying resources) that TAs can do to help teachers prepare for meeting the needs of pupils with physical needs in classrooms.

Preparedness for TAs with pedagogical roles

Training

The aim of any training considered here is to raise the quality of TAs' contributions to pupils' learning and academic progress. The audit process will show the range of qualifications and skills held by your TAs. As well as helping with your deployment decision-making, the audit may have revealed gaps in training for TAs and, most likely, teachers too. You should seek to implement a comprehensive and coherent whole-school strategy to address these gaps. As we have made clear, it is a mistake to take steps to change TAs' levels of preparedness without facing up to the implications for teachers. Some training can be aimed at both groups of staff, while other courses, sessions and interventions can be targeted at one group, or even at individuals. So even though this chapter does not expressly deal with how you might meet the training needs of teachers, there may be some things you develop for TAs that will also apply to teachers.

Developing TAs' subject and pedagogical knowledge

Few would argue that subject knowledge and understanding are fundamental to effective teaching; therefore, any deficit in the TAs' subject knowledge highlighted via the audit must be met with action of some kind. Indeed, Ofsted inspectors expect TAs to have sufficient subject knowledge so they are more able to promote thinking and learning through their interactions with pupils (2011b).

For TAs with a pedagogical role, quality training in teaching will also be necessary, so that they are better equipped to convey their knowledge to pupils. The comment below from one of the TAs involved in the EDTA project evokes the dangers of the 'training trap':

> *I don't know whether they think, because we did Insets on certain things, and they may cover that subject for half a morning, that's sufficient enough – which it clearly isn't. Maybe that's what they think. But me personally, I don't think it's enough. If you want me to do interventions, send me on a course. It's as simple as that.*
>
> Primary TA

Historically, the need for TAs to have pedagogical skills has been neglected. The DISS project made clear the effects of untested assumptions about how easily TAs would be able to take on the role of the teacher. Teaching is a highly skilled process and it is unfair to TAs, and to pupils especially, to expect TAs to develop these skills without specific preparation. If 'sitting by Nelly' can lead TAs to become as equally skilled as teachers, imagine the seismic – not to mention worrying – ramifications for the future of teacher training and the teaching profession at large.

Much of what TAs require in terms of developing both their subject and pedagogical knowledge can be achieved through in-house training. You could, for example, introduce regular informal 'mini-tutorials' for TAs, where teachers can brief them on topic information or technical processes (e.g. performing more complex mathematical calculations). This could extend to 'question and answer' sessions, where TAs can meet with subject teachers to get guidance and advice on concepts and processes. Teachers can use these sessions to keep up to speed on TAs' working knowledge and to check their understanding of the syllabus and instructional techniques.

The schools that participated in the EDTA study successfully delivered in-house training in order to improve the levels of TAs' subject knowledge and pedagogical skills. The schools drew on the expertise of teachers and TAs, to share good practice and to provide guidance and support through peer observations and feedback, which they found both valuable and cost-effective.

Training for TAs in how to manage interactions with pupils, how to select and use effective strategies for learning, and how to help pupils when they are stuck is crucial, and have been generally lacking in any formal and consistent way. As we have suggested, it is not enough to expect TAs to absorb these skills by simply sitting in the classroom and watching the teacher teach. We have already drawn attention to the amount of time TAs spend in a passive role, listening to teachers deliver their input to the class, but teachers in the EDTA project found that these moments can become valuable training opportunities. Before the lesson, teachers in the EDTA project directed TAs' attention to specific techniques that they then modelled in their whole-class input and which they wanted TAs to use when they supported a group later in the lesson. This classroom-level strategy can be developed into a consistent school-wide approach and enshrined in your school policy.

Of course, it might not be possible or practical to meet all training needs for TAs through in-house training. External training provision may be necessary, particularly in preparing TAs to support and interact with pupils with particular types of SEN, or to develop their subject knowledge and/or pedagogical skills, perhaps with regard to a curriculum intervention. Continuing professional development (CPD) that leads to qualifications and accreditation should be available and will formalise the acquisition of new skills. In a similar way to how Advanced Skills Teachers provide a benchmark for teaching quality, so qualifications earned through training can do likewise for TAs, as well as enhancing their confidence and self-image.

Training for TAs who lead classes

In Chapter 3, we explored the role of TAs leading classes, as part of school arrangements to release teachers for PPA and/or to cover short-term teacher absence. If you choose to deploy TAs to lead classes you need to ensure that they have the skills and training to succeed. Again, a programme of in-house training should be developed to ensure that TAs are given quality training from experienced teachers in classroom management skills. The role and the training will be framed by the expectations set out in the school policy on the appropriate use of TAs to work in place of teachers. Monitoring and mentoring should also feature as crucial elements of the training programme, so that TAs are supported in the early stages.

Key recommendations for preparing TAs with pedagogical roles

- Consider cost-effective in-house approaches to developing TA subject and pedagogical knowledge (e.g. mini-tutorials, observations), so they are more easily able to promote thinking and learning through their interactions with pupils.
- Ensure that TAs with a role leading classes receive training in classroom management and are supported by wider school systems.

Induction and performance review

Induction

We have heard anecdotally of TAs receiving highly questionable forms of induction, which consist of little more than reading pupils' individual educational plans and statements of SEN, or looking through resources packs and material from intervention programmes; although even this is better than nothing, which again has been the experience of some TAs we have met. Similarly, teachers have told us that even if they received some form of induction on appointment, it rarely included anything substantive on what the school expected from them in terms of TA deployment.

Newly appointed TAs and teachers should, therefore, receive a full school induction into the school's perception of all aspects of the work done by TAs.

The school policy on TA deployment is a useful vehicle for structuring induction and training around what the school expects from new teachers, and what new TAs can expect from teachers, in terms of being adequately prepared and deployed for pedagogical tasks.

Valuable models of school induction we have encountered include opportunities for new TAs to shadow experienced and effective TAs. If this is extended to new teachers as well, this form of shadowing will help new staff to have a better understanding of what the policy means in practice. Furthermore, through lesson observations, new appointees will also be exposed to what the school regards as exemplary teacher-TA collaboration in lessons.

New staff could also sit in on teacher-TA planning and feedback meetings to see how lesson plans are used and shared, once again becoming familiar with what kinds of practice the school will expect them to adopt.

One method of induction training that some schools in the EDTA project were seeking to develop involved the use of video recordings.

Case study

Watching and discussing a video of an experienced, effective TA in action

Teachers and TAs from one school watched a video recording of a TA colleague working with a group of pupils in a science lesson. This provided a useful springboard for a discussion about effective TA practice, which included how the TA used her time in the session and the instructional techniques she used.

Introduction to the school policy, shadowing TAs and observing teacher-TA meetings and lessons (live or on video) should be discussed afterwards to ensure that the intended outcomes have been achieved. The significant points related to being properly prepared need to have been identified and understood if you are to achieve consistent school-wide practice.

New teachers and TAs should be observed in the early stages of their employment, in order to get feedback on their performance and guidance for further development. Such comments on the performance of their roles can also be used to reassure them and you that the school TA policy is being used correctly and effectively. It can also reveal aspects that have been overlooked or misunderstood. Feedback depends on some form of monitoring of teachers' and TAs' preparation. You and your SLT may choose to do the monitoring, or you may delegate it to staff with particular responsibility and expertise.

Performance review and audit cycle

Of course, monitoring the work of new staff is not a one-off event. As new teachers and TAs become established members of your school workforce, they will become part of the annual performance review process. Their performance with regard to how they uphold or are supported by the school's policy on TA deployment and preparation should form part of their overall evaluation of performance. In particular, this will have greater implications for teachers, whose decision-making regarding TAs will be under scrutiny, than for TAs, whose effectiveness is determined by these decisions.

In Chapter 2, we set out the case for a whole-school audit on the deployment and preparation of TAs, much of which also applied to teachers. We also suggested that the audit can be used to review the implementation of new models of TA deployment, preparation and practice. Indeed, the audit could be used annually (maybe not in full, but at least components of it) to help you update your records on TAs' qualifications and training.

The regular audit cycle is intended to maintain the identification of training needs and the SLT should make provision for the necessary updating of staff knowledge and skills. Training must be ongoing, reacting to needs as they arise and new demands that may have to be met, for example when a pupil with a particular type of SEN previously not catered for joins the school.

Attempts to reverse the commonly found situation with respect to pupils with SEN will require concerted and systematic action at the school level. The school policy on TA deployment must address this and if required, training for teachers must be made available.

Key recommendations on TA induction and performance review

- Introduce a formal programme of induction for new teachers and TAs on TA deployment, structured around the school policy on TAs.
- Induction training could include the opportunity to shadow an experienced, effective TA.
- Ensure that new teachers and TAs receive support and guidance in the early stages of their employment.
- Use the auditing tools to carry out an annual review of how the school policy on TAs is being implemented, and to identify and meet gaps in staff members' knowledge and skills.

Day-to-day preparedness

One of our main recommendations based on the DISS project findings was that the day-to-day preparation for TAs must improve. Three-quarters of teachers we surveyed had no allocated time to meet with TAs. This situation must improve if schools are serious about TAs having a positive impact on learning outcomes.

The audit will have revealed the picture in your school regarding the opportunities available for teachers and TAs to meet, and the quality of lesson preparation. It is very likely that there will be echoes of the DISS project findings in what the audit reveals. If this is the case, you will need to develop and implement a school-wide strategy to formalise the ways in which teachers and TAs communicate.

Creating time for teachers and TAs to meet

We know from the DISS project that TAs are generally underprepared for the tasks teachers ask them to do daily, which means that it is essential to make changes to what TAs do with their time.

The audit will reveal the answers to three key questions and provide the starting point for reform:

1 How much time, if any, do your teachers and TAs have in which to meet?
2 If they have time, is this used effectively to brief TAs on lessons and receive feedback on lessons?
3 If they do not have time to meet, how are teachers' plans, tasks, expected outcomes for the lessons, *and* the role of the TA in the lesson, communicated to TAs?

The DISS project revealed the widespread lack of time available for teachers and TAs to meet before and after lessons for planning and feedback. If teachers and TAs in your school do not have time set aside in their hours of employment to meet, then you must change something to make such meetings part of the routine pattern of teacher-TA collaboration. Furthermore, the DISS study also showed that TAs worked, on average, an additional three hours voluntarily each week, spending much of that time in discussion with teachers. Many headteachers we interviewed were aware of how this could easily be seen as exploitative, though few had sought to do anything about it as the school relied quite heavily on TAs' goodwill: without it, there would be no teacher-TA meetings at all.

Present arrangements have to move away from the commonly found practice of using TAs' own unpaid time to hold planning and feedback meetings. If the school chooses to use TAs to teach, then surely it must take steps to allow them to be adequately prepared for the work teachers ask them to do with pupils. Similarly, if pupils are taught by TAs away from the classroom and teacher, then feedback is even more essential for assessment and planning purposes. There is a clear need therefore to formalise teacher-TA liaison time, so that overall practice can improve and the school can improve the effects of TAs on pupil learning.

Many school leaders and teachers we have spoken to maintain that in order to get 'best value' from their TAs, they should be spending every working moment with pupils. However, the findings from the DISS project suggest that the types of deployment and practice in operation are doing more harm to pupils' learning than good. Therefore there is a strong case for using part of the TAs' time each week for planning and preparation, so that they can be more effective the rest of the time when they are supporting and interacting with pupils. If, for example, TAs lead interventions, consider the added value that will be derived from providing dedicated time for them to plan and prepare thoroughly for these sessions. After all, if schools withdraw pupils from classes for curriculum interventions, every effort must be made to ensure that TAs are properly prepared in order to help them to make the accelerated progress pull-out programmes are designed to achieve.

Creating the kind of time we are referring to is most effectively achieved by extending TAs' existing hours of work, and that of course, costs money. We would be the first to admit that most school leaders would feel that in the current economic climate, this is a remote option. As we have mentioned, it was a deliberate part of the EDTA project design to encourage schools to think creatively within existing resources. Changes in the TA deployment did not depend on increases in funding, and so whatever schools achieved should be sustainable beyond the life of the EDTA study.

Some of the schools in our study looked for spaces in the school day where teachers and TAs could meet. Teachers and TAs met during assembly times, or during part of teachers' PPA time. Some schools, notably primary schools, were already doing this prior to the EDTA study.

Case study

Adjusting TAs' existing working hours

One primary school brought the start and finish times of the TAs' days forward by 15 minutes in order to create guaranteed time for the teacher and TA to discuss what the class were going to do each day and what roles the teacher and the TA would take in the lesson. This time also provided the opportunity for the TA to feed back anything from the previous day.

Both the teacher and the TA described this arrangement as 'invaluable'. This trial had been so successful that the school had decided to change the working hours of all its TAs in the same way. The governing body approved and from the start of the following school year, all teachers and TAs had daily liaison time.

Some schools acknowledged that changing TAs' contracts and hours of work was necessary for a significant improvement of TAs' level of preparedness. One possibility is to retain the same number of contracted hours, but to shift the start and end times, allowing teachers to have a set time for meeting TAs, at the start or the end of the school day. If you possibly can, increase the TAs' hours specifically to provide time to meet teachers. Both options will send out a strong and clear message: you are serious about ensuring that TAs are better prepared to teach pupils in your school.

It is important for you and your SLT to actively monitor the teachers' actual *use* of this time. Simply providing a space in the school day does not guarantee that teachers will know how to make best use of this precious time. At the outset, you should therefore make known your expectations about how the time should be used.

If TAs have a pedagogical role, using planning time to wash paint pots or do photocopying for the teacher on a regular basis does not represent best use of the time you have created. You need to be clear about how the time should be used effectively, and if necessary provide specific suggestions, guidelines or models to assist teachers. The broad intention of setting such time aside is to raise TAs' levels of preparedness, with the expectation that this will improve their interactions with pupils (see Chapter 5) and, in turn, raise pupil attainment. This is the point that needs to be emphasised and reiterated.

Developing a lesson plan template

One way of formalising what you expect teachers to provide in terms of TA preparation is to develop a lesson plan template that specifically requires teachers' to set out their instructions to TAs. The template will prompt teachers to give adequate thought to what TAs will do during lessons and what they need to know in order to do it effectively. The template should appear in your school policy on TAs, again acting as a reminder of how serious the school is about preparing TAs for teaching. It might be possible to set this template up in an electronic format enabling documents to be shared and modified more easily. It would also be possible for this kind of system to be interactive, with TAs adding comments and feedback. We will discuss lesson planning and feedback in more detail later.

Preparation for TAs who lead classes

Our research has shown that the effectiveness of TAs who lead classes, and cover supervisors working in a similar role, is heavily dependent on the quality of lesson planning and information sharing. But the DISS project also revealed other factors that can have an impact. We found that many teachers avoided planning demanding lessons for planned absences, which is understandable given the expertise required to deliver them. However, teachers instead supplied pupils with 'busy work'. When the tasks failed to engage pupils, there was a knock-on effect with poor behaviour. TAs and cover supervisors were left having to manage misbehaviour brought about by poorly planned lessons.

We present some more detailed guidance on preparation for TAs who lead lessons in the next section on class-level decision-making, but as a school leader, you will need to address this form of preparation at the school level and build it into your school's policies. In fairness to TAs undertaking lesson cover, they should not be sold short by inadequate lessons planned by teachers. You will need to decide the appropriate lesson format and tasks that teacher should be required to provide for TAs for planned absences.

Of course, a very regular feature of the cover supervisor's role, and one that we know extends to TAs, is that of covering an unplanned teacher absence. Realistically, an unplanned absence is less easy to prepare for on a day-to-day basis, so you will need to think about how you will handle this as a school. Again, the role of the TA covering the lesson and the lesson content should be consistent with the expectations set out in the school policy, so that the lessons run smoothly and are productive.

Year group leaders or subject department leaders could consider building a bank of activities suitable for cover lessons. These lessons should require little specialist knowledge or teaching. These could be group-based activities, which give pupils the opportunity to work together with minimal adult support.

TAs should only be used to cover lessons for the three consecutive days of an absence (WAMG 2008), so that, in a secondary school, the effects of this are unlikely to be damaging to pupils' learning in the long term. However, in a primary school, you should limit the use of TAs to cover whole days of absence, and instead bring in a supply teacher.

Key recommendations on the day-to-day preparedness of TAs

- Schools should make whatever adjustments are possible to suit the implementation of effective models of preparation, including adjusting TAs' existing working hours and/or contracts.
- Look for creative ways to timetable periods in the school day for teacher-TA liaison.
- Formalise the way teachers plan and share information about lessons by instituting a school-wide lesson plan template.
- Set standards or minimum expectations for what you expect from teachers in their lesson plans for lessons covered by TAs. Keep this under review.

Classroom-level decisions on preparedness

The guidance contained in this section is aimed at teachers, although it expands and develops some of the guidance above for school leaders in relation to lesson planning. In this section we will concentrate on the day-to-day aspects of preparation for TAs in pedagogical roles, as this is most relevant to class teachers. The main messages concerning the preparation of TAs deployed in non-pedagogical roles, and training for pedagogical roles (in terms of subject and pedagogical knowledge) is covered in the previous section, and so are not repeated here.

Day-to-day preparedness

Lesson planning

Our research has shown us that schools do not have a shared and consistent approach to lesson planning when it comes to defining the role and tasks of TAs, and sharing lesson plans. In any given school, it is likely that there will be teachers who do and teachers who do not; and the *quality* of preparation provided by those who do is often varied. By and large, we found that TAs acquire the knowledge they need for the lesson by tuning into the teacher's delivery. Many teachers argue that this is a form of preparation, but this is more like improvisation than planning and a misuse of valuable lesson time. As one TA involved in the EDTA project put it:

There is an assumption that you should just know. You're to come into a classroom, you listen to the 20 minutes of teaching, and from that – if you didn't know, you should know now. And then you're to feed it to the children. It's scary.

Primary TA

Making the best use of TAs requires you to think carefully about how you build the TA into your lesson and communicate this to them. As well as arming TAs with the requisite subject and pedagogical knowledge, you will need to ensure that you plan lessons with an awareness of what it is you specifically want them to do. You must provide TAs with explicit roles and tasks. Merely listing the names of the pupils assigned to the TA, for instance, can no longer be seen as enough. Equally, writing the TA's initials alongside things on the lesson plan more relevant to your role as a teacher is not sufficient.

Your lesson plans should make your intentions explicit and remove the need for the TAs to work out what was in your mind, or interpret notes on your lesson plan. It is too easy to assume that TAs have access to the implicit knowledge you hold as a practitioner. Therefore, you need to challenge how you communicate your lesson intentions and content to TAs.

Your overview of the curriculum, the extent of any unit of work, and the sequential development of concepts and understanding, all contribute to your understanding of a lesson plan. TAs tend not to have the same level of pedagogical awareness of the context in which any lesson plan can be set.

Ofsted inspectors expect you to be clear about what you want pupils to learn, and TAs must know too (2011b). Your lesson plans need to provide TAs with detailed and clear information about the tasks given to them about: the concepts, facts, information to be taught; the skills to be learned, applied, practised or extended; and the intended outcomes, in terms of products and learning.

As we will explore in the following chapter on TA practice, your plans should include questions and strategies for TAs to use when teaching individuals or groups. Consider the needs of the supported pupils and match TAs' tasks more closely to their needs, especially if they are lower-attaining pupils or have SEN. Also, be clear about how tasks can be sequenced and the time available in which to complete them.

If you are deploying a TA in a pedagogical role, this will involve supporting pupils. However, there may be other tasks that you wish TAs to carry out in a lesson, which should be made clear on your planning. You may want the TA to observe and record pupil performance or engagement for assessment purposes.

As we have stated, creating time for teachers and TAs to meet to plan and prepare lessons is the ideal situation your school should be aiming for. However, as a class teacher, you have little control over such top-level decisions. Furthermore, you will be aware of the implications of using the goodwill of your TA to create meeting times. So, if having additional time with your TA is unlikely, how can you make the most of the time that you do have?

Teachers and TAs who participated in the EDTA project found that where time to meet was limited, the teacher's lesson plan could act as the primary mechanism for communicating lesson aims to TAs. The plan was also used as the basis for the brief conversations at the start of the lesson. Having received the lesson plan in advance, the TA was able to clarify any points he/she did not understand, and the teacher was able to inform the TA of any changes to the plan. This avoided the TA having to interpret lesson plans without guidance from the teacher, which is the common experience of many TAs who are fortunate to see plans prior to lessons.

You must share your lesson plans with TAs at the earliest opportunity, in order for them to read and understand what you require from them and to get back to you with any queries. It is true, of course, that plans may change after you have shared them with the TA, but such tweaks will be easier to convey to TAs once they have an awareness of the overall aim and content of the lesson.

Case study

Using teachers' plans to identify where guidance was needed

One secondary school TA used the teacher's long-term plans to see which science topics and lessons were coming up. She was able to identify early on any gaps in her knowledge. The teacher expressed how useful it was for him to know the limitations of the TA's knowledge, and he took responsibility for explaining trickier concepts to individual pupils, rather than expecting or assuming that the TA could do it.

Preparation for TAs who lead classes

As we have noted, teachers failing to plan adequately often put TAs and cover supervisors who lead lessons in difficult situations: pupils disengage if given 'busy work', and can cause more disruption if bored or under-stimulated. Classes become harder to control – a situation exacerbated by the fact that pupils know that it is a TA in charge, rather than someone they see as having more authority. If there are behaviour incidents during a lesson as a result, this may mean work for you on your return if you have to investigate and deal with these incidents.

This is not a satisfactory position in which to put a colleague, so your planning for TAs leading classes in your absence should be annotated with specific instructions, or even written afresh with the TA in mind. You should ensure that the TA is aware of where to find any resources that are required. Think of any circumstances that could occur for which the TA would need to be ready; leave nothing to chance! If you know in advance which TA will be taking your lesson, seek them out and brief them on your lesson plan. Let them know about any particular pupil needs (for example, those who might need an extra explanation or those who are likely to be unsettled by the lesson being led by someone other than you).

In the EDTA project we found that that there were positive effects of improving the quality of lesson plans and sharing them with TAs prior to lessons. However, in order to give some flavour of the profound change that is possible, here are two comments from a TA and teacher pair:

I think with [teacher] sharing the lesson plans … I'm just noticing I feel more confident with the way I deal with the pupils, because I feel more secure in what I'm expected to do. Sometimes you know, occasionally when you come in cold, you feel unsure and you don't know what to say to the children so much … So I think sharing the learning objectives and what needs to be achieved and who to focus on, just means I'm much more aware of where to be.

Primary TA

I think the benefits outweigh any extra work ... I think to start with, it's a short-term steep learning curve, and then when you actually see the benefit and you think, 'how could I ever go back?' No way. I couldn't at all actually.

Primary teacher

Key recommendations on the day-to-day preparedness

- Be clear about the role you want the TA to take in your lessons, whom they are to support, what tasks they are to support, and what the expected outcomes are. Share lesson plans prior to lessons, and use time before lessons to discuss amendments.
- Share any strategies, techniques or key vocabulary you want TAs to use by modelling them in your whole-class teaching.

Teachers' engagement with interventions

In the previous chapter, we argued for greater involvement of teachers in the planning and assessment of curriculum interventions led by TAs. When teachers are more aware of what pupils are learning in these sessions away from the classroom, they are in a better position to integrate this into their planning for whole-class teaching and classwork.

The DISS project findings have shone a light on the ways intervention programmes are implemented and on the assumptions schools have made about their effectiveness. If TAs are to continue to deliver interventions, challenging your assumptions about the adequacy of their preparedness to do so effectively is vital.

The common practice of someone (usually not class teachers) handing over a pack containing an intervention programme and all the supporting materials to a TA cannot be assumed to be a sufficient form of preparation. There is, after all, more to teaching and learning than just working through a pack of materials prepared by someone remote from the school, with no knowledge of the individual pupils and their particular learning needs. Few teachers would accept this mechanical content delivery as a defensible model of effective teaching.

In line with our guidance on TA preparation for lessons, you need to satisfy yourself that TAs have a firm grasp of the purpose of each intervention programme they deliver and the tasks of which they are comprised. TAs will also need a range of effective strategies to use when responding to pupil errors and signs of struggle. As well as assessing the learning and the work from interventions, you must keep the TAs' effectiveness in using the intervention programmes under review. Therefore, interventions should form the focus of planning and feedback conversations with TAs.

As we explained in our earlier discussion of the DISS project findings, where teachers have no involvement with interventions, it means that what pupils do during the intervention sessions with TAs remains separate from what they learn in class with you. Pupils are left to apply their out-of-class learning to in-class contexts, which some will find demanding, if not impossible.

When you have greater awareness of pupils' learning from interventions, you can draw on concepts, facts, skills and understanding developed in the intervention sessions into your lesson planning. This will greatly enrich the learning experience of pupils receiving interventions, building on and making relevant the time spent out of class.

Furthermore, if you have some say over which interventions are run and how, you can organise things so that the interventions build on and complement what you are teaching in class. This will make the task of bridging that much easier for you, the TAs and the pupils. Pupils with learning difficulties often require material reiterated and reinforced to help them to understand content and skills, and require extended opportunities to practise them. Greater integration of your planning for whole-class lessons and interventions will maximise what can be achieved in TA-led interventions sessions, and will make classroom learning more meaningful for the pupils involved.

Case study

Integrating interventions with classwork

One TA had a heavy responsibility for leading intervention programmes for pupils in Year 3 and Year 6 classes. She explained that the Year 6 maths content matched what the pupils were doing in class with their teacher, and that the teacher knew the learning objectives and sequence of lessons in the intervention programme. This allowed her to synchronise and integrate learning from the two contexts. In contrast, the Year 3 teacher knew nothing of the intervention programme that the TA led with pupils from her class and so there is no integration of learning.

Key recommendations on improving teachers' engagement with interventions

- Increase your familiarity with the interventions used in the school.
- Through your conversations with TAs, find ways to integrate the content and learning from interventions with your class teaching. This will allow you to check pupils' understanding, reinforce learning and give professional input where needed.

Feedback from TAs

As will now be clear, feedback from TAs on their role in lessons and interventions, and on the engagement and progress of pupils, completes the preparation loop. It is this information that informs your understanding and interpretation of pupil work and behaviour, and in turn, your future lesson planning.

As Ofsted (2011a) noted, outstanding practice demonstrates marking and dialogue between teachers and TAs of a consistently high quality. To enable this, you should provide a steer to TAs about what constitutes relevant and useful feedback. Left to them, there is no guarantee that TAs will know exactly what constitutes worthwhile feedback. Clear guidance will help to structure the content of the TAs' feedback to you, whether this is in verbal or written form.

In terms of pupil engagement and learning, it should be clear that feedback from TAs should be linked to the learning objectives. Feedback should be more developed for responses that indicate poor engagement or lack of progress. You will need to know whether the task you set was well targeted, clearly defined and/or adequately differentiated, and whether the teaching approach used by you and/or the TA was appropriate to the task.

Feedback from TAs is necessary for monitoring TAs' understanding of tasks, as well as pupil outcomes. You can gain insights into how TAs interpret the tasks you gave them, which can be used to address any misunderstandings or limitations in their perceptions of the work. Similarity, feedback provides a check and balance for confirming TAs' understanding of lesson content (e.g. facts and concepts).

As we have mentioned, the quality of feedback, as much as planning, is partly dependent on the time available for it. However, try to do all you can to obtain regular feedback from TAs. The benefits to you and your lesson planning are considerable if you can tap into the detailed knowledge of pupils that TAs pick up in every lesson. You need to provide the structure to facilitate this, but once it is in place, it can become a routine and valuable part of your week.

Teachers in the EDTA project found that feedback was most effective when TAs had been given clear directions from teachers on what they wanted them to feed back, and when feedback was linked to lesson objectives.

The favoured mechanism for enabling feedback is teacher-TA dialogue. This was certainly the chosen method used by the participants in the EDTA project. However, written forms of communication also featured, particularly in secondary schools. Several teachers included a designated space on their lesson plan in which TAs could provide any comments. This was seen as a way of overcoming the lack of time to give feedback face-to-face. We saw that one possibility for the future is more electronic forms of communication between teachers and TAs.

Case study

Written forms of feedback

Teachers in one primary school developed a shorthand system for using in pupils' books. As one teacher explained: *'A full triangle [means] … that they could do it all independently, by themselves; [TA] didn't need to really support them. Two sides [∧] means they needed a little bit of support to get going, but they've grasped it; they just need to build their confidence. And one side [/] means they need a lot of support; they can't do this by themselves.'*

Feedback is a type of summary, but the value for you lies in the detail, as this can be used to inform your further lesson planning.

> *If [TA] has worked with a certain group … She'll assess [their work] and focus [feedback]. She'll tick which part's right … and then she'll have discussion with me and I'll say 'How did your group get on?', and she'll pinpoint kids who didn't get to it, or the ones that did and need reinforcement. And then I'll be able to see that as well from her marking.*
>
> Primary teacher

Key recommendations on feedback from TAs

*   Be specific about what you want TAs to feed back to you after a lesson, especially if time is tight.

- Aim to supplement written feedback with brief discussion.
- Use this feedback to inform your future lesson planning.

Summary

The schools and teachers that participated in the EDTA project successfully addressed many of the issues raised in the DISS project concerning the day-to-day aspects of TA preparation. We end this chapter with a brief summary of the key findings:

- The creation of time for teachers and TAs to meet had a positive effect on participants' perceptions of TA preparedness.
- Primary schools created teacher–TA liaison time by reconfiguring TAs' hours of work. Finding time to meet was a greater challenge for secondary schools.
- The quality and clarity of teachers' lesson plans improved and reduced instances of TAs going into lessons blind or relying on picking up information via teachers' whole-class delivery.
- Involvement in the project had the effect of instigating a rigorous performance management process for TAs.

Chapter 5

The practice of TAs

Introduction

The quality of verbal interactions between adults and pupils is at the heart of effective teaching and learning. This chapter focuses on TA-to-pupil interactions (or what we call 'practice').

The DISS project found that schools were largely unaware that TAs' interactions with pupils tended to focus on task completion rather than understanding, and that, compared with teachers, TAs asked more closed questions and fewer open questions, thereby closing down learning opportunities. Schools were equally unaware of the problems TAs faced when it came to carrying out the tasks delegated to them by teachers. Consequently, teachers and schools were generally unable to detect possible limitations, or even damage, to pupils' learning and progress.

There is clearly a serious gap in some schools regarding knowledge about the quality and effectiveness of TA practice that cannot remain unchallenged. Having made decisions about the pedagogical or non-pedagogical role of TAs, you will need to address how this manifests itself in terms of TAs' interactions with pupils, the nature of the talk, the things they say, etc.

If you have decided to give TAs a non-pedagogical role, then their verbal interactions with pupils should serve to aid learning *indirectly*. However, it is highly likely that interactions that seek to nurture, encourage, motivate and manage behaviour inevitably overlap with aspects of teaching and learning. Complete separation is, to an extent, artificial or theoretical in the pragmatic reality of the classroom.

However, there remains a clear and major distinction between TAs with teaching roles, for whom it is necessary to have interactions concerning subject content and learning, and TAs employed predominantly in a non-pedagogical role, who have a different, but complementary, impact on learning.

If you have decided that TAs will have a pedagogical role in your classrooms – working directly with pupils, delivering and supporting curriculum content – then the issue of TAs' practice must be addressed in a serious and systematic way. The key question to begin with is: how much do you already know about the nature and quality of TAs' interactions with pupils?

As is clear from the guidance in Chapter 2, some form of auditing should precede any changes to TAs' practice. Fundamentally, this would involve some form of listening in on the verbal interactions of TAs with pupils. The insight obtained by such close attention to TAs' talk is both essential and extremely valuable. Effective changes aimed at improving the quality of TA talk – that is, making it more effective in promoting pupil learning – will only be possible if you are well enough informed about present practice.

In this chapter, we look at decision-making concerning TAs' practice – the final main component of the Wider Pedagogical Role model. Given that the guidance in this chapter is applicable at both the school and classroom level, we will not distinguish between the two levels. However, we will draw readers' attention to guidance that is specifically directed at school leaders.

We will first consider the implications for practice for TAs in non-pedagogical roles, and then for those in pedagogical roles. The majority of the guidance in this chapter concerns the latter.

Some important questions to ask about TA-to-pupil interactions

- *How much do you already know about the nature and quality of TAs' interactions with pupils?*
- *Do you attempt to monitor TAs' conversations with pupils and their use of questions?*
- *What would you do if you discovered that TAs frequently provided pupils with answers, or misled them (unintentionally) with inaccurate information?*

TAs with non-pedagogical roles

If a decision has been made to deploy TAs in ways that support pupils' learning indirectly (that is, TAs are not expected as a matter of course to have instructional interactions with pupils), this should be reflected in the expectations regarding their talk to pupils. Furthermore, the decision to deploy TAs in this way, and what this means for their interactions, should be clear to pupils.

In Chapter 3 we considered three roles for TAs for which role demarcation is necessary and should be reinforced through TAs' interactions with pupils. First, we suggested an in-class behaviour management role for TAs, dealing with low-level disruption. If this is the chosen role for your TA(s), you must develop appropriate forms of talk relating to dealing with pupil behaviour, consistent with the ways in which teachers deal with behaviour. In this sense, TAs overlap only with teachers' classroom management function, and not with their pedagogical function.

The second role we looked at was TAs supporting pupils with physical needs. We know that problems often occur when the interactions of TAs with roles supporting pupils with physical needs (for example, TAs who sign for hearing impaired pupils) stray into teaching. The boundary, therefore, must be clear. In the case above, the TA providing signing can interpret the teacher's talk, but should not be expected to teach the pupil herself. Again, the roles of the teacher and the TA are clear and distinct, but complementary.

As we explained in Chapter 3, the third TA role is more niche, as it has far less to do with the pedagogical role of mainstream teachers. TAs deployed to support pupils' emotional needs deliver specific interventions. The interaction skills TAs require to work effectively in these roles can be acquired as part of formal training to deliver these programmes (see Chapter 4).

TAs with pedagogical roles

There are two dimensions of TA talk that emerged from the EDTA project:

- Effective questioning skills,
- Supporting and developing pupils' independent learning skills.

TAs' questioning skills

The interactions between adults and pupils are at the heart of learning, and a large part of these interactions involve questioning. Asking questions to engage and promote learning is a skilled task. Such pedagogical questions are generally categorised as closed or open, or as lower order or higher order, with open and higher-order questions regarded as the most effective types of talk (see Table 2.9 in Chapter 2).

The DISS project findings revealed that pupils are engaged in sustained and active interactions with TAs far more often that they are with teachers. But the analyses of adult-to-pupil talk (including questioning) conducted as part of the study also showed that there are marked differences in the quality of TA-to-pupil interactions when compared with teacher-to-pupil interactions. TA talk is of a poorer quality, it is less cognitively demanding, and prioritises task completion over learning and understanding.

As questioning is such a significant means of developing pupils' thinking, aiding the growth of their conceptual knowledge and understanding, extending their critical thinking skills and for checking their learning while engaged in tasks, there should be a concerted drive to improve TAs' questioning skills. Ofsted have made it clear in their guidance to inspectors with the responsibility for assessing SEN that input from TAs should promote thinking and learning as opposed to task completion (2011b).

If your audit reveals that TAs' talk is characterised by closed and lower order questions, you will need to take action to raise the quality of their questioning skills. Of course, we acknowledge that closed questions do have their place in teaching, but you should be alert to their overuse or use where an open question is more appropriate to the task.

Many of the participants in the EDTA project admitted at the outset to giving little consideration to TAs' questioning techniques:

> *Without realising it I was quite often using closed questions ... A lot of the time, because the kids that I'm working with often struggle, you just want them to feel like they're progressing or achieving. But actually when you think about it, for that minute or second when you've virtually given them the answer they might be feeling a bit better, but if you look at the big picture, it's not helping their progress.*
>
> Secondary TA

If you recognise this situation, you will need to raise the awareness of the importance of questioning, provide TAs with models of good practice, and support them in developing their questioning skills.

Raising awareness

Skilful questioning to aid learning is at the heart of teaching, and by its nature, is a two-way transaction, attempting to lift the lid on the workings of the pupil's mind, to reveal to both the teacher and the pupil, just what is known, how much is properly understood, and where any barriers to learning may be. This is the vital role of questioning, and until it is brought to their attention, most TAs may be unaware of its importance and how demanding it is to handle effectively. Understanding the value of questioning must therefore extend to TAs.

If you are a school leader, consider training all TAs in effective questioning techniques, and if you or a member of the SLT can lead this training, it will leave TAs (and teachers) in no doubt about its seriousness and value. The key is for TAs to develop an understanding of questioning techniques that help to push pupils on. What is required is very clear, practical advice and guidance on what effective questioning looks like and when it should be applied.

Case study

Focusing on the importance of quality questioning

One primary school put a deliberate focus on questioning, which sent out a powerful message about the esteem in which the school held it. The deputy headteacher led training for TAs on suitable questioning techniques. These techniques complemented the questioning techniques used by class teachers. Pairs of TAs observed one another in action, working with pupils, and made notes for a feedback discussion. TAs appreciated the opportunity to learn from one another and develop new skills and strategies.

Developing models of good practice

Teachers are well placed to provide TAs with models of good questioning via their whole-class input. TAs are familiar with listening to teachers teach and some have no doubt picked up useful skills from their observations; however, many TAs may engage superficially with what they see and hear in the classroom. The deeper intentions, selection of forms and various uses of the questions – tacit as they are to teachers – are less likely to be understood by TAs.

Opportunities to model good questioning practice and formative assessment techniques are available every time a TA works in a class with a teacher. As we suggested in the chapter on TA deployment, if teachers are clear about what they want TAs to do at different stages of the lesson, they can create the opportunity for TAs to observe their whole class input and take note of particular techniques they use, which TAs can use later as they support individuals or groups.

Teachers will need to be clear about which techniques they want TAs to adopt in, say, their group work, because not all forms of questioning teachers use in their whole-class talk will be relevant to contexts in which TAs mainly work. Teachers could therefore arrange for TAs to observe them working with individual pupils and groups, and model effective questioning on these contexts.

TAs should note the variety of questions and the use of thinking time, and use this to reflect on their own practice. Attention can also be given as to how teachers manage instances where a pupil does not know the answer, or gives an incorrect or incomplete answer, and how the teacher stimulates and prompts pupils to generate ideas.

Case study

Modelling questioning

One primary school TA observed the teacher working with a pupil with SEN on a one-to-one basis. The teacher's interactions involved a lot of questioning, probing and scaffolding. The teacher and TA discussed the observation afterwards. The TA had gained useful insights into working effectively with pupils one-to-one. She identified instances where the teacher's actions had been particularly effective and different to what she would have done. For example, the TA noted how the teacher gave the pupil time to respond to her questions; the TA realised that she did not tend to do this.

Resources

Questions for TAs to ask pupils can be included in the teacher's lessons plans and given to the TA in advance. Teachers could also prepare questions or prompts linked to subjects for TAs to use in class. Some teachers in the EDTA project provided TAs with frameworks of different types of questions and prompts designed to facilitate learning and critical thinking, with examples, some of which were based on Bloom's taxonomy. With the kind permission of the teachers who developed them, we have reproduced these resources in Appendices 3 and 4.

Case studies

Avoiding unproductive questions

One teacher gave her TA written guidance on avoiding unproductive questions, which err towards spoon-feeding, 'over-prompting' and task completion. In this way, the TA was as aware of less effective techniques as she was of effective techniques. Some further examples are provided below:

Try to avoid:

- *Recall questions* to which the answer is obvious
- *Rhetorical questions* solely for dramatic effect
- *Yes or No questions* that inhibit discussion
- *Leading questions* that are not open-ended
- *'Guess what I'm thinking' questions* where you've already formulated the answer you want
- *'Why don't you try …' questions* that supply alternative answers or ideas

Using a question bank

TAs and teachers in one school used a question bank – a laminated resource listing categories of useful questions. Use of the question bank encouraged greater variety in questioning techniques with pupils. Members of the SLT had referred to the bank during observations, helping to gauge TAs' range and use of questions.

   TAs in another school used a similar resource, developed by a secondary school English teacher. The teacher encouraged teachers and TAs across the department to use a prototype version, and used their comments and feedback to produce an improved version.

Questioning frameworks and printable resources developed by teachers are freely available on the internet without copyright. We provide an example of a simple-to-use question matrix drawn together from these various resources in Table 5.1. Questions of increasing complexity can be constructed using a word from further down the left-hand column and a suffix from further along the top row. For example, comprehension questions beginning with 'who is' or 'what did' are of a lower order than questions beginning with 'why would' or 'how might', which invite speculation.

Table 5.1 Effective question matrix

	Complexity					
	Is ...	Did ...	Can ...	Would ...	Will ...	Might ...
Who						
What						
Where						
Why						
When						
How						

(left axis labelled *Complexity*; top axis labelled *Complexity* with arrow)

As TAs develop their questioning skills over time, and this becomes a regular feature of their practice, there will be less need to provide detailed direction. Teachers' plans could simply reference the appropriate set or type of questions for any lesson or any pupil.

Embedding and sustaining practice

It should be noted that developing effective questioning skills is not easy. The TAs in the EDTA project recognised that developing more effective questioning skills required undoing old habits. Asking closed questions was an ingrained practice, as was the tendency to jump in automatically with additional questions, rather than allowing time for a pupil to respond to the first question. Therefore, schools and teachers must recognise this and monitor TAs' progress. They should follow up initial training with further opportunities to practise and ongoing mentoring and support. Such training and support should also be part of the school induction programme for new TAs.

TAs should be encouraged to appraise their own practice critically and have open discussions with teachers aimed at developing a shared understanding of the purpose of talk and the desired outcomes – in particular, that it is acceptable for pupils not to finish a task, in favour of talk that advances pupil learning. This was certainly something of a revelation for the participants in the EDTA project, who, once exposed to the findings from the DISS study, were convinced of the need to eradicate ineffective and unhelpful forms of interaction, and replace them with more constructive models. As a result of the development work on bringing attention to less effective types of talk, one TA acknowledged that it is difficult to break the habits she had got into regarding her choice of questioning. But as she explained, she was more aware of the types of talk to avoid: '*I caught myself saying [to a pupil] the other day, "Why don't you use x word, instead of y word?" And I think, 'Oh God, I shouldn't be saying that!*'

Finally, once the practice has become embedded, school leaders should ensure that the use of questioning is reviewed as part of TAs' annual performance appraisal. This will send out a strong signal that the school expects TAs to demonstrate effective use of questions in support of pupils' learning.

Key recommendations on TAs' questioning skills

- Make a concerted drive to ensure that TA-to-pupil interactions promote thinking and learning, rather than task completion.

- Raise awareness among both teachers and TAs of the importance of quality questioning.
- Teachers need to share their tacit knowledge and skills relating to effective pupil interactions with TAs via training, observations and discussions.
- Ensure that teachers explicitly model key techniques in their whole-class input, so that TAs' practice can be consistent with teachers when supporting pupils.
- Produce resources with exemplars of quality questioning and formative assessment techniques.
- Monitor and support TAs as they develop new questioning skills. Provide guidance and mentoring and opportunities to practise.
- Encourage TAs to become reflective practitioners, and develop strategies in partnership.
- Include a review of TAs' questioning skills in their annual performance appraisal.

Supporting and developing pupils' independent learning skills

A job of any school and teacher is to develop pupils' skills for thriving in school and beyond. Nurturing the development of 'soft skills', such as confidence, motivation and positive dispositions towards learning and attempting new things – learning to be independent and self-reliant – are all important for lifelong learning. But to what extent do TAs share and support this goal?

Much research, including the DISS project and research by Michael Giangreco in the USA, has revealed the unintentional, but nonetheless, damaging effects of pupil dependency on TA support. The DISS study showed that TAs can provide pupils with answers, and are most concerned with task completion, and this can lead to pupils becoming dependent; relying on the TA to do the work for them.

Participants in the EDTA project recognised the need for TAs to be included in the drive to enhance pupils' ability to work independently, and for their interactions with pupils to serve this aim, rather than work against it. They also recognised that TAs are already well placed to be able to do this, in terms of having regular, sustained and active interactions with pupils. However, what needed to be changed was their use of language.

Improving TAs' questioning skills will help you to develop pupils' thinking skills, but you will also need to develop complementary models of talk that help pupils to become independent learners. Such forms of TA talk will be particularly useful for TAs who are deployed to lead classes. As pupils have to be more self-reliant in such contexts, it is important that they have the skills for taking ownership for their learning in the absence of the teacher.

Again, you will need to raise the awareness of the importance of developing pupils' independent learning skills, provide TAs with models of good practice, and help them to hone these skills.

Raising awareness

In much the same way as we have explained the necessity in relation to developing TAs' questioning skills, you will need to draw attention to the need for TAs to play a key role in fostering pupil independence. If you are a school leader, make this issue the subject of a meeting or training session for teachers and TAs. Discussion should emphasise the importance of developing resourceful, lifelong learners, both in terms of the benefits to the individuals themselves and to society in general.

If your school runs an expansive education programme, such as *Learning to Learn, Building Learning Power* or *Enquiring Minds*, and TAs are not familiar with the aims of the programme, you may be missing an opportunity to support the development of pupil independence.[9]

Case study

Including TAs in expansive education programme

One secondary school ran an initiative called *Building Learning Power*. BLP is a programme aimed at creating a culture of teaching and learning that systematically cultivates habits and attitudes to enable pupils to face difficulty and uncertainty calmly, confidently and creatively. At the start of the EDTA project, it was discovered that TAs were somewhat detached from the aims and teaching techniques used by BLP practitioners. The school held training for TAs and teachers encouraged and supported TAs to use and develop these skills in their interactions with pupils.

If the drive to improve pupil independence is backed up by the very obvious commitment and involvement of SLT, then TAs, along with all the teaching staff, will realise the importance the school is attaching to it. If linkages can be made between improved grades and the ability to learn independently, this will increase commitment.

If you are a class teacher, you will already be aware of how your decisions about TA deployment in the classroom can directly affect the pupils' independence (see Chapter 3). Routinely deploying TAs to work with the same (often lower-attaining) pupils makes your expectations of such pupils clear: this pupil is not capable of independent learning, so must be propped up by an adult. Inevitably, the pupil subconsciously believes this to be true and soon becomes dependent on the TA. Deploying TAs in alternative ways (e.g. strategic withdrawal of TA support at appropriate moments) emphasises the value of and creates the conditions for pupils thinking and acting for themselves.

Developing models of good practice

We have found that many TAs have never before been given permission to depart from the default practices into which the majority have settled. As you develop models of effective practice, you will need to instil a new culture that can set TAs free from the patterns of thought underpinning less effective practice.

A good example of this is 'stereo teaching', which is the term we used to describe the effect of how intermittent talk from the TA to pupils during the teacher's delivery to the whole class can effectively separate the pupils from the teacher; the pupil hears two adult voices, very often saying the same thing – hence the stereo effect (for more, see Blatchford, Russell and Webster 2012). TAs often talk when they do not need to in order to justify their presence in the classroom. If they are listening to the teacher teach, and have not said anything for several minutes during this time, their sense of needing to do something builds.

Similarly, TAs often describe a sense in which teachers judge their effectiveness in terms of the quantity and/or quality of work produced by the pupils they support during a lesson.

This often leads TAs to take on too much of the task, spoon-feeding answers and reducing the opportunity for pupils to think and work independently.

In both cases, TAs feel compelled to act in the interests of the pupils they are supporting. However, in these particular circumstances, greater educational benefits are likely to flow if the *do not* act. This is counterintuitive, of course, but the evidence from the DISS project is clear on the effects of these types of TA-to-pupil interaction.

TAs need to be freed from this restrictive behaviour. They need to know that it is acceptable for them to deprioritise task completion in favour of more beneficial learning experiences. Schools and teachers need to make it clear to TAs that it is preferable to act in ways that enable pupils to attempt tasks independently, than to ensure that there is some tangible outcome that can be shown to the teacher at the end of the lesson. It is better that a pupil completes three or four sums and understands the methods of calculation than produces a completed worksheet of correct answers, spoon-fed by the TA, and learns nothing about the process by which they were derived.

It is important to develop models of good practice. An initial step is to identify existing good practice and formally share this with TAs. As we have already mentioned, good teachers do know the strategies and techniques for promoting pupil independence, but such knowledge needs to be made explicit for TAs.

Directing TAs' attention to forms of speech used by teachers to promote independence is another way of making tacit knowledge visible. In much the same way as we have described developing effective questioning skills, teachers could model techniques in their interactions with pupils. The TA's observations can form the basis of a follow-up discussion to understand and refine practice.

Knowing what to do when you do not know what to do

The essence of developing pupils' independent thinking skills is to inculcate a particular habit of mind, summed up best by paraphrasing Jean Piaget's definition of intelligence: knowing what to do when you do not know what to do. The role of TAs with pedagogical responsibilities should be to help pupils to help themselves, consistent with the 'guide on the side' view of teaching. While teachers have the primary responsibility for equipping pupils with the tools to think through ways in which to tackle new problems, TAs can assist by prompting pupils of certain steps to take to help them do this.

There is real value in developing forms of TA talk that serve this particular form of pedagogy, as do they not require any specific subject knowledge and are thus transferable between a multitude of contexts. Whether a pupil is stuck in history, maths, French or textiles, the formula for working through a problem is roughly the same: reflecting on one's existing knowledge; drawing on one's experience; looking for clues in the current situation; and using other resources and tools (e.g. the internet) to find the answer.

The role of the TA in such circumstances is to help pupils internalise and practise these valuable skills of self-sufficiency. Schools and teachers can work through examples of what this type of talk looks like and the particular questions or phrases that are appropriate at certain moments. These forms of talk have much in common with higher-order questions. Examples could be collected and collated to produce resources for TAs to use, as already suggested for questioning skills. Such examples (some of which we heard TAs use in an EDTA project school) include:

- *What's your plan?*
- *How can you find out about ...?*
- *What do you notice about ...?*
- *What do you know already that could help you?*
- *What happened when you got stuck before?*
- *How can you use what you learned last week to help you here?*
- *What can we use to help us with this?*
- *Who else could help you?*
- *What would help you avoid distractions?*
- *What could you teach me about ...?*

Some of the teachers in the EDTA project explored the use of pupil-led strategies to promote independent skills. Some introduced self-help strategies, for which there is a clear logic: in order to develop the skills for independent thinking, pupils need to be independent and not have recourse to adult support. Other teachers used peer tutoring and peer supports. Both models have the effect of moving away from the tendency for adults to be the first resort for assistance, not the last.

Case studies

Pupil self-help strategies

One primary school introduced classroom rules for independent learning. When stuck, pupils were expected to work through a sequence of strategies for tackling problems – re-reading the question, asking a friend for help (but not the answer!) before asking an adult for support.

Encouraging pupils to think

Another primary school TA was encouraged to turn pupil requests for assistance towards the rest of the group, thereby prioritising peer support over adult support. She also reflected questions back to the pupil, in order to stimulate his/her own thinking. This practice also ensured that the pupil retained the responsibility for his/her own learning.

TAs and collaborative group work

In the DISS project we were struck by the way that TAs did not always appreciate the tacit intentions behind group work and TA involvement in group work could work against the overarching aims of independent learning. To be fair, research conducted in the Social Pedagogic Research into Group-work (SPRinG) project, co-directed by Peter Blatchford, found that teachers themselves did not always see the benefits of collaborative groups for pupils, and had difficulties in setting up good quality group work. We found that working effectively with groups required a rethink from the usual way adults worked with pupils – a move from an obviously interactive role to something more like the 'guide on the side' role already referred to. One of the main benefits of group work is that it can allow pupils to learn from each other (e.g. through the exchange of ideas, having to justify and explain points of view, developing new explanations, and so on). The value of group work is likely to grow as we move from education as the imparting of knowledge to one in which there is far more assessing and evaluating of evidence that is widely available.

We found in the SPRinG project that setting up good quality group work required careful support from teachers, careful preparation of the classroom and the tasks, and careful training of pupils in ways of working in groups. Given that many teachers tell us they have difficulties with group work, it is not surprising if TAs also have difficulties. In particular, we have found that the 'guide on the side' approach, recommended for much group work, which deliberately allows pupils more control over their learning, is difficult for TAs, who can feel obliged to interact with pupils and, as a result, hinder independent learning.

We, therefore, recommend that TAs need to be prepared for supporting pupil groups. As with other areas, TAs would need to be shown explicitly how to work with pupils and shown how to step back to allow pupils more control over their own learning.

Readers may find this book helpful: *Promoting Effective Group Work in the Primary Classroom: A handbook for teachers and practitioners*, by Baines, Blatchford and Kutnick (2008).

Embedding and sustaining practice

Our research has revealed that TAs have little or no choice about the ways in which they are deployed. Our wider understanding of the TA role shows that this is a historical development, which has remained unchallenged for years.

As with developing effective questioning skills, it will take time for TAs to adopt the forms of talk aimed at promoting pupils' independent thinking skills, and gain the confidence to make judgements about when to withdraw from pupils and when to return.

TAs will need help in changing ingrained habits, which takes time and support. Some TAs have a controlling and intrusive manner, so changing to act in a more 'hands off', facilitative way will require training, guidance and plenty of opportunities to practise.

New ways of working that encourage pupils to become independent learners may challenge teachers, as well as TAs. If you are a school leader, ensure that you allow all your staff time to adjust to the new practices, and support them as they change their professional routines and relationships. It will be worthwhile, as the approaches we have outlined should, in time, provide you with a much more effective TA workforce, contributing to, rather than undermining, the development of confident and independent lifelong learners.

Key recommendations on supporting and developing pupils' independent learning skills

- Whole-school initiatives to develop pupils' independent learning skills must include an appropriate role for TAs.
- Instil a culture that sets TAs free from unhelpful patterns of thought that underpin less effective types of talk.
- Develop forms of talk that help pupils to know what to do when they do not know what to do.
- Ensure that teachers explicitly model key techniques, so that TAs' practice can be consistent with teachers'.
- Produce resources with exemplars of techniques.
- Consider the use of pupil-led strategies (self-help and peer supports) as an alternative to adult support, and ensure that pupils retain responsibility for their own learning.

- Allow time for these new practices to take effect.
- Monitor and support teachers and TAs as they develop new questioning skills. Provide guidance and mentoring and opportunities to practise.
- Ensure that TAs do not hinder pupils' independent thinking in group work, and consider a school-wide drive towards effective support for group work, which includes TAs.

Chapter 6

Conclusions

Summary of the Effective Deployment of Teaching Assistants (EDTA) project

This book was written to address the startling results from the Deployment and Impact of Support Staff (DISS) project: pupils who received the most support from TAs made significantly less progress than similar pupils who received less support (Blatchford, Russell and Webster, 2012). The DISS project showed that this troubling and surprising finding is explainable in terms of the ways TAs are actually deployed in schools. The extensive observation and other forms of data collection in the DISS project showed that at present TAs often have a frontline pedagogical role, but an ineffective one. Problems emerge particularly when TAs are given an ill-defined remedial role. We concluded that the impact and practice of TAs need to be seen in terms of decisions made about their deployment, preparedness and their conditions of employment – things that are outside their control. We called for a fundamental reassessment of the way TAs are used in schools.

This was the background to the Effective Deployment of TAs (EDTA) project, which took place between 2010 and 2011, and is the basis of this book. The aim was to develop alternative strategies to the three main components of the Wider Pedagogical Role (WPR) model: TA preparedness, deployment and practice. National, large-scale research, followed by a coherent and empirically sound explanatory model, was used as the basis for a collaboration with schools on the development of key recommendations.

We are confident that if the ideas and suggestions in this book are used, there will be a considerable improvement in the use of TAs and, importantly, the educational experiences and learning of pupils. In the EDTA project we found there was a good deal of productive work over the school year, in all three components of the WPR model.

With regard to *deployment*, at the school level, senior leadership teams (SLTs) thought more strategically about the purpose of the TA role and expectations in terms of pupil outcomes. Many conducted some form of audit of current practices to establish the need for, and the extent of, change required. Overall, attention had been turned to how TAs could 'add value' to the teacher's role rather than replace it.

Schools formalised new models of TA deployment and implemented wider changes for the following school year (2011/12). In some schools, TAs were used as 'advocates for change', selling the benefits of doing things differently to the wider school staff. Overall, schools had challenged entrenched, unhelpful mindsets towards the use of TAs and provision for pupils with SEN.

There were also marked and productive changes to the deployment of TAs at the classroom level. TAs worked more often with average- and higher-attaining pupils, and teachers spent more time with lower-attaining and SEN pupils. This greatly improved and enriched teachers' understanding of these pupils and their needs. Careful thought had been given to less productive uses of TAs; for example, teachers reduced the proportion of time in which TAs were passive during lessons, and TAs more often remained in the classroom, thus reducing pupil-teacher/pupil-peer separation. In line with recommendations by Michael Giangreco and colleagues (2004), attention had also been given to alternatives to adult support, for example, through peer supports, collaborative group work and 'self-help' strategies.

In terms of *preparedness*, schools found that creating time for teachers and TAs to meet had a positive effect. Primary schools created liaison time by changing TAs' hours of work, though this was still a challenge for secondary schools. The quality and clarity of teachers' lesson plans improved and plans were shared with TAs and supplemented with daily discussion, which made explicit the role and tasks of the TA for each lesson. Involvement in the project also encouraged many schools to instigate performance management processes for TAs.

With regard to *practice*, there was good work at the school level on changing TAs' talk with pupils. This included encouraging TAs to consider when *not* to talk, thereby giving pupils time to respond. Perhaps for the first time, TAs were encouraged to adopt the pedagogical goal that interactions with pupils should be about understanding, *not* task completion. TA practice developed to support formative assessment and expansive education initiatives. At the classroom level, there were two key developments: first, questioning frameworks to help pupils remain in charge of and responsible for their own learning; and second, strategies to help pupils become independent learners, thereby reducing dependency on adult support.

A final word on TA-to-pupil talk

In the last chapter on 'practice' we concentrated on just two aspects of TA-to-pupil talk that emerged from the EDTA project as particularly significant in schools. There are of course other aspects of instructional talk to pupils that fall outside these two dimensions. The interactions teachers have with pupils, and the language they use, have long been recognised as playing an important role in pupil learning. There are inevitably different views on what constitutes effective teaching, but it is possible to identify a number of common features from research (see Rubie-Davies *et al.* 2010):

- Effective teachers spend time orientating pupils to lessons and making links to prior learning.
- New concepts are introduced by providing high levels of instructional talk and checking pupil understanding; and effective teachers ask far more questions that require pupils to reason and engage in higher-level thinking.
- Effective teachers frequently provide pupils with feedback about their learning and encourage them to participate.
- For talk to promote pupil learning and conceptual understanding actively, effective teachers clearly articulate concepts and ideas, and skilfully scaffold pupil learning.

A consideration of this list makes it clear just how skilful teaching is, and how challenging it is for TAs when they are assigned a pedagogical role. It seems fair to say that in many schools we have allowed TAs to take on a frontline pedagogical role, but have not really considered the nature of the talk that takes place. This presents a dilemma, which we feel it is important to bring out. Is it realistic to expect TAs to talk to pupils in the same way as teachers, informed by the same degree of training in subject and pedagogical knowledge? Can we really expect TAs to use talk in service of the kinds of effective teaching already summarised? If not, then what do we expect from TAs?

Work on types and styles of questioning and developing pupils' independent working skills are important, but more general solutions to the appropriate role of TAs in interactions with pupils still need attention. In conjunction with our colleague Julie Radford at the Institute of Education, London, we have begun work on a more general way of analysing classroom talk. This allows us to position TA-to-pupil talk relative to teacher-to-pupil talk in such a way that it identifies distinctive but different contributions.

In general terms, we suggest it would be very helpful if the teacher developed a clear view of the type of talk they want the TA to stress in any given lesson or session, in relation to the particular task that has been set, and encourage them to use it with pupils. In this way, for example, the TA can play an effective role in developing pupil thinking and conceptual development, without necessarily having the full subject knowledge of a teacher (Radford *et al.* in press).

Final comment

A constant refrain in this book is that, in order to bring about the necessary change, it is important that the whole school is involved and that leadership comes from the headteacher and the SLT. It is not enough, as some headteachers have assumed, to assign the job of reform to the SENCo or other member of staff, especially if they are not members of the SLT.

We have found that engaging in the work described in this book has been professionally important for all staff. Teachers became more aware of their responsibilities to pupils and TAs, and it was clear that the TAs who took part felt more valued, appreciated, and more confident in their role and abilities.

Appendices

Appendix 1. Survey pro forma

A note on using the survey pro forma

We have collated the example survey questions set out in Chapter 2 into a photocopiable pro forma. If you chose to give this to staff as part of your audit, we encourage you to provide a cover letter informing them of its intended use and communicating instructions for completion and return. You may also like to add your own open-ended questions; some suggestions are given in Chapter 2. We recommend that audits are completed and returned anonymously. We recommend that audits are completed and returned anonymously – though you will need to identify which audits have been issued to teachers and which to TAs. Include a space at the top of the audit sheet for respondents to write their role title.

1. Working in the classroom (to be completed by teachers and TAs)

1.1 During a typical school week, estimate the proportion of time (as a %) that you spend doing the following. Only provide a percentage score for item 6 if you are a TA. Ensure that your percentages add up to 100%.	
1) Working with a pupil one-to-one	%
2) Working with a small group (up to 5 pupils)	%
3) Working with a larger group (between 6 and 10 pupils)	%
4) Roving the classroom	%
5) Leading the class	%
6) (TAs only) Listening to teacher talk to the class	%
7) Other (please specify)	%
Total	100%

1.2 During a typical school week, estimate the proportion of time (as a %) that you spend doing the following. Ensure that your percentages add up to 100%.	
1) Supporting higher-attaining pupils	%
2) Supporting average-attaining pupils	%
3) Supporting lower-attaining pupils	%
4) Supporting pupils defined as having SEN (e.g. those with a statement of SEN)	%
5) Supporting mixed attainment groups	%
Total	100%

2 Working away from the classroom (to be completed by TAs only)

2.1 During a typical school week, estimate the proportion of time (as a %) that you spend doing the following. Ensure that your percentages add up to 100%.	
1) Working with a pupil one-to-one (e.g. leading an intervention)	%
2) Working with a group of pupils (e.g. leading an intervention)	%
3) Working with pupil(s) in a pastoral/welfare context (e.g. mentoring; physio)	%
4) Preparing, planning and/or assessing pupil work (including for interventions)	%
5) Doing administrative tasks (e.g. photocopying or filing for teachers; display)	%
6) Other (please specify)	%
Total	100%

2.2 During a typical school week, estimate the proportion of time (as a %) that you spend doing the following. Ensure that your percentages add up to 100%.	
1) Supporting higher-attaining pupils	%
2) Supporting average-attaining pupils	%
3) Supporting lower-attaining pupils	%
4) Supporting pupils defined as having SEN (e.g. those with a statement of SEN)	%
5) Supporting mixed attainment groups	%
Total	100%

For the following eight sections, tick the statement that best matches your experience.

3. Pre-lesson preparation

3.1 Opportunity for teacher-TA communication	✓
1) No opportunity/time to communicate before lessons	
2) Communication before lessons is brief and ad hoc	
3) TA comes in early/stays behind after school to meet with teacher for briefing	
4) Teacher and TA have scheduled time to meet (e.g. time for which TA is paid)	

3.2 Quality of preparation for TA (teachers' lesson plans)	✓
1) TA goes into lessons blind. No lesson plan provided	
2) TA given lesson plan. No specific information about TA role given	
3) TA given lesson plan. Limited information about TA role given (e.g. pupil names)	
4) TA given lesson plan. Specific information about TA role given (e.g. objectives/outcomes)	

4. Post-lesson feedback

4.1 Opportunity for teacher-TA post-lesson communication	✓
1) No opportunity/time to communicate after lessons	
2) Communication after lessons is brief and ad hoc	
3) TA comes in early/stays behind after school to meet with teacher for debriefing	
4) Teacher and TA have scheduled time to meet (e.g. time for which TA is paid)	

4.2 Quality of TA feedback to teachers (written/verbal)	✓
1) TA does not feed information back to teachers	
2) TA feeds back basic information (e.g. 'task completed'; 'pupils on-task')	
3) TA feeds back detailed information (e.g. specific problems with/progress towards learning goals)	

5. Interventions

5.1 Preparation for interventions: guidance from teachers	✓
1) TA plans and prepares interventions, with very little/no input from teachers	
2) TA plans and prepares interventions, with some general guidance from teachers	
3) TA plans and prepares interventions, with substantive, detailed guidance from teachers	

5.2 Feedback on interventions: quality of TA's feedback to teachers (written/verbal)	✓
1) TA does not feed information back to teachers	
2) TA feeds back basic information (e.g. 'task completed'; 'pupils on-task')	
3) TA feeds back detailed information (e.g. specific problems with/progress towards learning goals)	

6. TAs' subject and instructional knowledge

6.1 Subject knowledge	✓
1) TA gains subject knowledge by tuning in to teacher delivery (e.g. as part of class audience)	
2) TA gains subject knowledge from lesson plans and/or schemes of work	
3) TA gains subject knowledge via ad hoc communication with teacher	
4) TA gains subject knowledge via substantive briefing/training from teacher	
5) TA has significant level of subject knowledge via specific training (e.g. TA has degree in subject)	

6.2 Instructional knowledge	✓
1) TA gains instructional knowledge by tuning in to teacher delivery (e.g. as part of class audience)	
2) TA gains instructional knowledge from lesson plans and/or schemes of work	
3) TA gains instructional knowledge via ad hoc communication with teacher	
4) TA gains instructional knowledge via substantive briefing/training from teacher	
5) TA has significant level of instructional knowledge via specific training (e.g. TA has QTS)	

Appendix 2. Observation pro forma

Date:		Teacher:		Lesson details:
Class/Year:		TA:		

Time (minutes)	Lesson part*	Predominant activity of TA					TA-supported pupil(s) (name, attainment level, SEN status)	Task differentiation for TA-supported pupils	Comments on teacher's role	Features of TA-to-pupil talk
		With pupil one-to-one	With group of pupils	Roving classroom	Listening to teacher teach	Other task (tidying/admin)				
1										
2										
3										
4										
5										
6										
7										
8										
9										
10										
11										
12										
13										
14										
15										
16										
17										
18										

Time (minutes)	Lesson part *	Predominant activity of TA					TA-supported pupil(s) (name, attainment level, SEN status)	Task differentiation for TA-supported pupils	Comments on teacher's role	Features of TA-to-pupil talk
		With pupil one-to-one	With group of pupils	Roving classroom	Listening to teacher teach	Other task (tidying/admin)				
19										
20										
21										
22										
23										
24										
25										
26										
27										
28										
29										
30										
31										
32										
33										
34										
35										
36										
37										
38										

Time (minutes)	Lesson part*	Predominant activity of TA					TA-supported pupil(s) (name, attainment level, SEN status)	Task differentiation for TA-supported pupils	Comments on teacher's role	Features of TA-to-pupil talk
		With pupil one-to-one	With group of pupils	Roving classroom	Listening to teacher teach	Other task (tidying/admin)				
39										
40										
41										
42										
43										
44										
45										
46										
47										
48										
49										
50										
51										
52										
53										
54										
55										
56										
57										
58										
59										
60										
Total ✓										
Summary		%	%	%	%	%				

* Key for Lesson part: I = Teacher's main input T = Main learning task P = Plenary

Appendix 3. Questions and key words for critical thinking

		Are you sure? How do you know? Can you tell me why?			
Remembering	Understanding	Applying	Analysing	Evaluating	Creating
You want to find out what the children know.	You want to find out what the children understand.	You want to support the child in solving a problem, using what has been learned.	You want to support the child to examine and break down information into parts.	You want to support the child in reflecting on and evaluating work and ideas.	You want to support the child to represent information in a new or alternative way.
Who ...?	Tell me in your own words ...	How would you solve ... using what you've learned ...?	What are the parts or features of ...?	What works/worked well?	What changes would you make to solve ...?
What ...?	Which is the best answer, and why?	What do you know already that could help you?	What is the theme ...?	What would you change?	Can you think of another way?
Where ...?	What facts and ideas show ...?	What other way would you plan to ...?	How is ... related to ...?	How could it be improved?	Can you predict/ estimate? What do you think it's going to be?
When ...?	How are these the same? Different?	What would happen if ...?	How could you sort these?	Do you agree with the actions ...? with the outcome ...?	How would you adapt ... to create a different ...?
Which ...?	What is the effect of ...?	What do you think you need to do next?	Why do you think ...?	What is your opinion of ...?	How could you put all your ideas together?
Why ...?	What is the main idea of ...?	How could you use what you've learned?	What evidence can you find to support this?	What information would you use to support these views?	
How would you show/ explain/describe ...?	What does this mean?		What conclusions can you draw ...?	How would you prove ...? disprove ...?	
			What is the function of ...?	What/which is the most important ... and why?	
				Why did they choose ...? How would you do it differently?	

Appendix 4. Prompts for facilitating learning and thinking

These prompts will help you to *facilitate* pupils' *learning* and *thinking* in lessons.

'*Telling them the answer is not always learning.*'

- Show me something that is solid.
- Can you tell me the equipment you have used?
- Find something that is used to make an electrical circuit.
- Having read the information, what is it telling you?
- Where can you find the meaning of the word?
- What does ... mean? Why has this happened?
- What could you say about ...?
- What might happen next? What do you see? How do you know?
- What is in the picture? Which ... go together?
- Can you explain? Are you sure this is true? How do you know?
- Where did you get the information from?
- How are you going to present the results?
- Explain the meaning of two key words.
- What have you learnt about ... today?

- *Have you given pupils time to answer the question?*
- *Are you allowing the pupils to work independently?*
- *Are you encouraging pupils to work in pairs or groups?*

Notes

1 This definition includes higher-level teaching assistants, nursery nurses, nursery assistants, literacy and numeracy support staff, learning mentors, foreign language assistants, special needs and minority ethnic pupils' support staff, plus any other non-teaching staff regularly employed to support teachers in the classroom.
2 All full-time equivalent teachers and support staff in publicly funded schools, including all local authority maintained schools, academies and city technology colleges.
3 A more in-depth presentation and analysis of the DISS project findings, thematically arranged to cover all components of the WPR model, can be found in our book: Blatchford, P., Russell, A. and Webster, R. (2012).
4 For further information, see Blatchford *et al.* (2008).
5 Digital voice recorders are relatively inexpensive items that can be purchased from online retailers, such as www.amazon.co.uk, for as little as £20 each. We have found that by using a tie clip microphone plugged into the recorder it not only makes for a better quality recording but is also more discreet; the recorder can be hidden away in a pocket. A tie clip microphone can be purchased online for less than £5.
6 For information on ELSA, visit http://www.elsanetwork.org
7 Structured conversations form part of the Achievement for All intervention package. For more on this, visit http://www.afa3as.org.uk
8 The freedom that schools have in order to apply such stipulations varies between local authorities. If in doubt, seek advice from your authority's human resources department.
9 Expansive education is an umbrella term describing teachers and schools that are committed to focusing on the development of useful, transferable habits of mind – alternatively defined by various programmes as 'capabilities', 'competences', 'attributes' and 'dispositions' – throughout mainstream education.

References

Alborz, A., Pearson, D., Farrell, P. and Howes, A. (2009) *The Impact of Adult Support Staff on Pupils and Mainstream Schools*. London: Department for Children, Schools and Families and Institute of Education.

Anderson, V. and Finney, M. (2008) '"I'm a TA not a PA!": Teaching Assistants Working with Teachers', in G. Richards and F. Armstrong (eds) *Key Issues for Teaching Assistants: Working in Diverse and Inclusive Classrooms*, pp.73–83. Oxon: Routledge.

Baines, E., Blatchford, P. and Kutnick, P. (2008) *Promoting Effective Group Work in the Primary Classroom: A Handbook for Teachers and Practitioners*. Oxon: Routledge.

Blatchford, P., Bassett, P., Brown, P., Martin, C., Russell, A., and Webster, R. with Babayigit, S. and Haywood, N. (2008) *The Deployment and Impact of Support Staff in Schools and the Impact of the National Agreement: Results from Strand 2 Wave 1 – 2005/06* (DCSF-RR027). London: Department for Children, Schools and Families.

Blatchford, P., Russell, A., Bassett, P., Brown, P. and Martin, C. (2004) 'The effects and role of Teaching Assistants in English primary schools (Years 4 to 6)' 2000–2003: results from the Class Size and Pupil–Adult Ratios (CSPAR) Project. Final Report (Research Report 605). London: DfES.

Blatchford, P., Russell, A. and Webster, R. (2012) *Reassessing the Impact of Teaching Assistants: How Research Challenges Practice and Policy*. Oxon, UK: Routledge.

Blatchford, P., Webster, R. and Russell, A. (2012) *Challenging the Role and Deployment of Teaching Assistants in Mainstream Schools: The Impact on Schools. Final Report on the Effective Deployment of Teaching Assistants (EDTA) project*. Online. Available at: www.schoolsupportstaff. net/edtareport.pdf (accessed 26.09.12).

Department for Education (2011) *Support and aspiration: a new approach to special educational needs and disability – A consultation*. London: Department for Education.

Department for Education (2012a) *Local authority and school expenditure on education, children's services and social care for 2010–11, including school revenue balances (OSR 03/2012)*. London: Department for Education.

Department for Education (2012b) *Statistical first release (SFR06/2012): School workforce in England (provisional) November 2011*. Online. Available at: http://www.education.gov.uk/ researchandstatistics/statistics/recentreleases/a00205723/school-workforce-in-england-pro visional-nov-2011 (accessed 14.05.12).

Department for Education and Skills (2003a) *Raising Standards and Tackling Workload: A National Agreement*. London.

Dunne, L., Goddard, G. and Woodhouse, C. (2008) 'Teaching assistants' perceptions of their professional role and their experiences of doing a foundation degree', *Improving Schools*, 11 (3): 239–249.

Ekins, A. (2012) *The Changing Face of Special Educational Needs: Impact and Implications for SENCos and their Schools*. Oxon: Routledge.

Fraser, C. and Meadows, S. (2008) 'Children's views of teaching assistants in primary schools', *Education*, 3–13, 36 (4): 351–363.

Giangreco, M.F. (2003) 'Working with paraprofessionals', *Educational Leadership*, 61(2): 50–53.

Giangreco, M.F. and Broer, S.M. (2005) 'Questionable utilization of paraprofessionals in inclusive schools: are we addressing symptoms or causes?' *Focus on Autism and Other Developmental Disabilities*, 20: 10–26.

Giangreco, M.F. and Doyle, M.B. (2007) 'Teacher assistants in inclusive schools', in L. Florian (ed.) *The SAGE Handbook of Special Education*. London: Sage, pp. 429–439.

Giangreco, M.F., Yuan, S., McKenzie, B., Cameron, P. and Fialka, J. (2005) '"Be careful what you wish for ...": five reasons to be be concerned about the assignment of individual paraprofessionals', *Teaching Exceptional Children*, 37(5): 28–34.

Gross, J. (2008) *Beating Bureaucracy in Special Educational Needs*. Oxon: Routledge.

Lamb, B. (2009) The Lamb Inquiry: Special Educational Needs and Parental Confidence. London: DCSF.

Muijs, R.D. and Reynolds, D. (2001) *Effective teaching: Evidence and practice*. London: Paul Chapman.

Norwich, B. and Lewis, A. (2001) 'Mapping a pedagogy for special educational needs', *British Educational Research Journal*, 27(3): 313–329.

Ofsted (2005) Managing challenging behaviour. London: Ofsted.

Ofsted (2011a) The evaluation schedule for schools. Guidance and grade descriptors for inspecting schools in England under section 5 of the Education Act 2005, from September 2009, Ref. no: 090098. London.

Ofsted (2011b) Special educational needs and/or disabilities in mainstream schools. A briefing paper for section 5 inspectors. London.

Radford, J., Bosanquet, P., Webster, R., Blatchford, P. and Rubie-Davies (in press) 'Fostering learner independence through heurisitic scaffolding: a valuable role for teaching assistants, International Journal of Educational Research.

Radford, J., Rubie-Davies, C., Blatchford, P., Russell, A. and Webster, R. (2012) 'The practice of TAs', in Blatchford *et al.* (2012).

Rubie-Davies, C., Blatchford, P., Webster, R., Koutsoubou, M. and Basset, P. (2010) 'Enhancing student learning? A comparison of teacher and teaching assistant interaction with pupils', *School Effectiveness and School Improvements*, 21(4): 429–449.

Scottish Government (2011) *Summary statistics for schools in Scotland, No.2. 2011 edition*. Online. Available at: http://www.scotland.gov.uk/Publications/2011/12/06114834/0 (accessed 14.05.12).

Statistics for Wales (2011) *First release (SDR 153/2011(R)): Schools' census 2011: Final results – revised*. Online. Available at: http://wales.gov.uk/topics/statistics/headlines/schools2011/110906/?lang=en (accessed 14.05.12).

Webster, R., Blatchford, P. and Russell, A. (2012) 'Challenging and changing how schools use teaching assistants: findings from the Effective Deployment of Teaching Assistants project,' School Leadership and Management, first published on 9th October 2012) (iFirst).

Wiliam, D. (2010) 'How should we use what we know about learning to read?' Keynote address at *'Changing Lives': 7th International Reading Recovery Institute*, at the Institute of Education, London, 8 July.

Workforce Agreement Monitoring Group (WAMG) (2008) *The appropriate deployment of support staff in schools*, WAMG Note 22, London. The WAMG Guidance for schools on cover supervision is available online at: http://www.lge.gov.uk/lge/aio/476204 (accessed 26.09.12)

Index

adding value to teaching 8, 59–60, 62–3, 69, 99

assumptions: about candidates for TA posts 58; about effectiveness of interventions 89; about support for pupils with physical needs 67; about TAs 11, 19, 80, 87, 89

audit 5, 7; consulting TAs 20, 39,102; features of 5, 16, 19–21; frequency of 40, 76–7; of skills and qualifications 35, 39, 45–7, 50, 71, 73

Baines et al 103

change: process/timescale/fundamental review of current practice/purpose and role of TAs 3, 5–9, 18, 41–3, 54, 58, 87, 99–101

classroom organisation 25, 42, 55, 65

conditions of employment: key recommendations 59; recruitment/job descriptions/entry qualifications 50, 57–8, 99; see also working hours

consultation 7, 24, 42, 44, 46–7

cost of TAs 52, 84

Cover Supervisors 59–60, 85–6, 88

curriculum coverage 18, 45

deployment of TAs 21, 100; hours of work 4, 57–9, 78–9, 86, 100; predominant activity 28, 30–3, 105–8; purpose of TAs 3, 23, 40–1; school policy on TA deployment 8, 42–4, 47, 49, 53, 55–6, 58, 62, 66, 73–7, 79–80; tasks 11, 13–14, 21–2, 25–7, 29, 39–43, 45, 47, 49, 60, 62, 68, 71–3, 75, 77, 80–1, 87, 100, 103; non-pedagogical roles 41–5, 47–8, 70–3, 80, 87–8; behaviour management 47, 49, 54, 60–2, 72–3, 75, 88; defining the non-pedagogical roles 60, 62; key recommendations 49, 62, 73; parent liaison 43, 47, 49; pupil support: direct 11, 14, 22, 41–3, 47, 87; indirect 22, 43, 60–1, 87–8; support for pupils with physical/emotional/pastoral needs 21–2, 26, 42, 45, 47–9, 61–2, 72–3, 88, 103; supporting teachers 21, 47, 60–2, 71–2, 87–8; pedagogical roles: 11, 14, 41–5, 50, 52, 57–8, 63, 73–4, 79–81, 87–8, 99–101; class-year-or subject-based 54–6, 65, 69; defining the pedagogical roles 41, 43–5, 49–50, 58, 62–3; deploy differently in three lesson phases 27–9, 67, 90; direct: adding value 8, 59–60, 62–3, 105; important questions to ask 43; key recommendations 44, 51, 56, 65, 75; passivity of TAs 30, 67, 69, 74, 100; TAs leading classes 53–4, 75, 82

Deployment and Impact of Support Staff in Schools (DISS) study: aims 1, 5; findings i, 1–4, 7–11, 13–15, 18–19, 29, 35–9, 41, 43, 45, 47–8, 50–5, 57–8, 60, 63–5, 68, 70–1, 74, 77–9, 83, 87, 89, 92–3, 95, 99

Effective Deployment of TAs (EDTA) project 15–20; adding value 69, 99; aims 25; evaluations 16; interventions 15, 28–30, 37, 57–8, 67, 74, 76, 78, 81–2, 85, 89, 91–3; key findings 17, 69, 86, 99; key recommendations 7–8; trials 16, 51, 56, 88, 95–6

effectiveness of TA support 54, 58, 68, 79

Emotional Learning Support Assistants (ELSA) 48–9, 72, 111

feedback time for TAs and teachers see preparedness

Giangreco 2, 10, 18, 47, 62, 93, 100

goodwill of TAs 13, 36, 78, 81

headteacher role 4–5, 8–9, 24, 28, 41, 44–5, 51, 54, 59, 73, 76, 79, 89, 91, 94, 99, 101

Higher Level TAs 6, 10, 24, 35, 45, 54, 57

impact of TAs on pupil learning 1–2, 6, 11–12, 14, 18–20, 37, 51, 61, 65, 77, 87, 99
independence of pupils: collaborative group work 96, 100; dependency of pupils on TAs 34, 44, 56, 62, 65, 69, 93–5, 97–8, 100; independent learning skills 9, 48, 64, 85, 88, 93–4, 96–7, 100–1, 110; key recommendations 97; raising awareness/ modelling/training 67, 82, 89, 93; self-help strategies 96, 100
induction 9, 57, 75–7, 92
Initial Teacher Training (ITT) 4–5, 8, 15, 71
Inset 3, 5, 13, 35, 74
interactions with pupils: TAs' 11–13, 88–9, 93; teachers' 12–13, 50, 64
interventions: asking questions 53; integration with class learning 38, 50, 52–3, 65–6, 83–4; key recommendations 53, 66, 84; teachers' engagement with 83–4

key recommendations 5, 99; adding value 60; class/year or subject based 56, 69; conditions of employment/recruitment 59; EDTA project 7–8; feedback from TAs 85; independence of pupils supported by TAs 97; induction/performance review 77; interventions 53, 66; non-pedagogical role of TAs 49, 62; pedagogical role 51, 65, 75; practice of TAs 92, 97; preparedness of TAs 73, 75, 80, 83; school level decisions 42; school policy on TAs 44, 46–7; TAs leading classes 54; TAs' questioning skills 92; teachers' engagement with interventions 84

lesson observation schedule (audit) 27–30, 33, 67
lower-attaining pupils see pupils with SEN

National Agreement 10, 45, 53

performance management of TAs 39, 57, 86, 100
planning lessons: communication of plans 9, 13, 17, 22, 36–40, 56, 70, 76–7, 80–3, 85–6, 91–2, 100, 103–4; lesson plan template 79–80; time for 2, 9, 12–14, 17, 29, 36–8, 42, 55–6, 77–81, 83, 85–6, 100
practice of TAs 2, 8–9, 16, 33, 99; features of TA to pupil talk 14, 29–34, 105–8; interactions with pupils 2, 5, 14, 17, 19, 29, 33, 35, 67, 74–5, 79, 87, 93–4, 100–1; key recommendations 92, 97; task completion 13, 34, 87, 89, 91–3, 95,100; teachers managing TAs 13, 39–40, 71; see also questioning

preparedness of TAs: day to day 4, 9, 12–13, 35–6, 43, 70–3, 77, 80, 86; feedback time 2, 9, 12–13, 22, 32, 36–8, 41, 53, 66–7, 72–3, 76–9, 83–6, 103–4; in-house training 74–5; instructional/pedagogical knowledge 13, 36, 56, 73–5, 80–1, 101; key recommendations 80, 83; planning time/pre-lesson communication 9, 13, 36–40, 56, 85, 103–4; subject knowledge 9, 38, 42, 56, 68, 73–5, 95, 101–4; see also training for TAs
Planning, Preparation and Assessment (PPA) time 29, 45, 78
pupils' academic progress i, 1, 4, 12, 15, 41, 44, 59, 73
pupils with SEN 2, 4, 7, 9–10, 12, 17–19, 23–4, 40; parental expectations 40, 49, 51; support from TAs 50–1, 56, 62–4, 66, 77, 99; teachers' knowledge of 24, 39, 50, 64–6; training for teachers 65, 70–1, 77

qualifications of TAs 11, 14, 35, 43, 46–9, 53, 56–9, 62–3, 73, 75
questioning 34, 88–9, 100; closed/open questions 23, 32, 34, 87, 89, 92; higher/ lower order questions 31, 34, 89, 91; key recommendations on TAs' skills 92–3; raising awareness/modelling 68, 89–91, 93; resources 91, 93; styles 9, 101; TAs' skills 88–90, 92–3, 98

school improvement 4–5, 7, 20
SENCo/inclusion manager 3–6, 8, 13, 15–17, 24, 35, 51, 66, 101
SEN Green Paper 17
separation of pupils: from curriculum 52, 63–4, 69; from peers 35, 51–2, 62–4, 69, 100; from teachers 4, 25, 50–2, 55–6, 62–4, 69, 73, 100

TA goodwill 13, 36, 78, 81
teachers: effective teaching 33, 73, 83, 87, 100–1; TAs as alternative to 50, 60, 63; switching roles with TAs 50, 64, 77; teacher's role 4, 8, 29–33, 38, 63, 68, 81, 94, 99, 105–8; job satisfaction 47, 60; knowledge of SEN 39, 71; preparation to manage TAs 39, 71; workloads 11, 47
training for TAs 2–3, 9, 12–14, 35, 38–9, 42–3, 46–9, 53–4, 56–8, 61–2, 65, 71–7, 80, 88–90, 92–4, 97, 101, 104; see also preparedness of TAs

working hours of TAs 4, 57–9, 78–9, 86, 100
Wider Pedagogical Role (WPR) model 2–3, 7–9, 11, 15, 19, 41, 57, 70, 99, 111